MW01621076

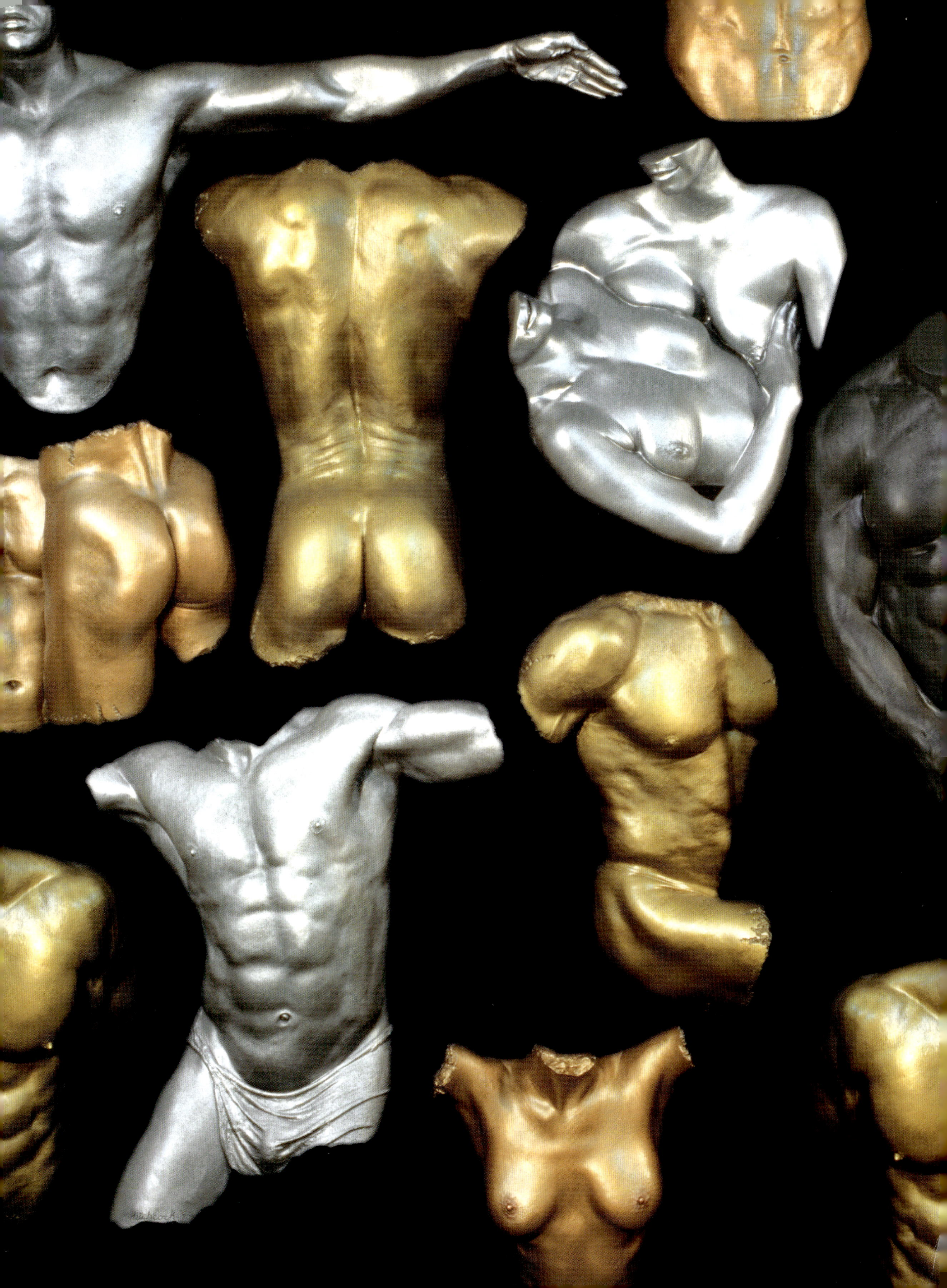

FRONT COVER:
ROBERT, 1996
cast gypsum, wood,
36” x 20” x 12”

FRONTISPIECE:
VARIOUS TORSOS, 1996
cast gypsum,
life size

Published by
ELLIS PUBLICATIONS
P.O. Box 5922
Santa Monica, CA 90409
ellispublish@earthlink.net

Library of Congress Card Number: 00-103573
ISBN 0-9700843-2-3
Printed in Korea

DARK IMPRESSIONS

The Art of Philip Hitchcock

ELLIS PUBLICATIONS

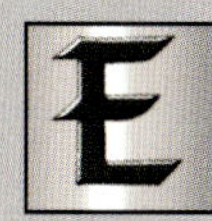

Regarding this body of work.....

I first came across the artwork of Philip Hitchcock in 1991. At that time he was involved in a showing of his work entitled “Queers on Crosses: A Homo Crucifixion.” The exhibition was held at, of all places, a funky little West Hollywood coffee house called *The Abbey*. The opening reception fell on good Friday and bread and wine were offered as hors d’oeuvres. The exhibit featured five, life size male torsos in white plaster and depicted various stages of bondage and crucifixion- including one which was strung up by his heels, one impaled with a spear, and one bound with ropes to a St. Andrews style cross! (all are pictured within) Such was my introduction to Mr. Hitchcock!

Although I came to know later, that many of his pieces possess an understated classical beauty, more than a few, like the ones just mentioned, are jarring, commanding images that at once frighten and captivate the viewer. While the casting technique provides for a sort of “hyper realism,” the very shape, form, and finish of the pieces are stylized; setting in motion another more subliminal tension that further disarms the onlooker. Exquisite layered finishes and glazes complete each piece and often secondary elements such as animal skulls, iron fittings and sections of cast resin are added. Ultimately you are rendered powerless by the sheer force of dignity that Hitchcock’s figures possess. This is not cerebral, high brow, conceptual art, but “stop-you-in-your-tracks-and-rush-over-to-see-kind-of-art!” You don’t need a decoder ring or any critics to translate. The feelings will wash over you.

The artist’s craftsmanship and technique are without parallel. It was a great surprise for me to learn that Hitchcock’s sculptures are often the amalgam of two or even three different models. Additionally, a finished sculpture might be cast in many sections and then painstakingly reassembled into its final form. There is very little in Hitchcock’s art that is random or accidental.

Dr. David B. Dearinger, the chief curator of New York City’s National Academy Museum and School of Fine Arts writes the following about Hitchcock’s work:

> “As an art historian and museum curator, I have been impressed with Mr. Hitchcock’s sculptures, both for their aesthetic merit and for the technical ability they display. Like the remnants of sculptures of ancient Greece and Rome which have come down to us, they blend a marvelous sense of the ideal and the eternal with a fragmented suggestion- or even reminder- of instability and temporality. At the

same time, their tendency toward eroticism, especially homoeroticism, make them very much a part of the modern world and give them appeal to modern sensibilities. Suggestions of bondage and struggle heighten their eroticism for the viewer or at least allow the viewer to interpret the works as expressions of psychological as well as physical states of being. In other words, like all masterworks of art, Mr. Hitchcock's sculptures lend themselves to several levels of interpretation.

I am also impressed with the process by which Mr. Hitchcock creates these works. Again like the ancient Greeks, he selects the best parts of individual bodies to achieve the ideal, molding his figures or parts from life. He then uses fine materials worked to exquisite finishes that give his sculptures their extremely realistic details but also enhance their idealism. In all these ways, his products continue to fascinate and, for their beauty, attract the viewer."

Having seen the artist's work in person and having visited his studio numerous times during the compilation of this book, I say with some trepidation that photographic reproductions cannot begin to do the work justice. But having come close to that impossible goal, the photographs in this book are shot by the artist himself and are exquisite two dimensional renderings that are nothing short of hypnotic. It seemed only logical to have Hitchcock design the book as well, making this, his first book, a definitive statement of the artist's body of work to date. I invite you to immerse yourself into what I'm sure will be an inspiring experience.

Arthur James

Senior Editor, Ellis Publications

FOOTSOLDIER, 1997

cast gypsum, resin, steel, sheep skulls,
32" x 24" x 14" *Model: Tony Powers*

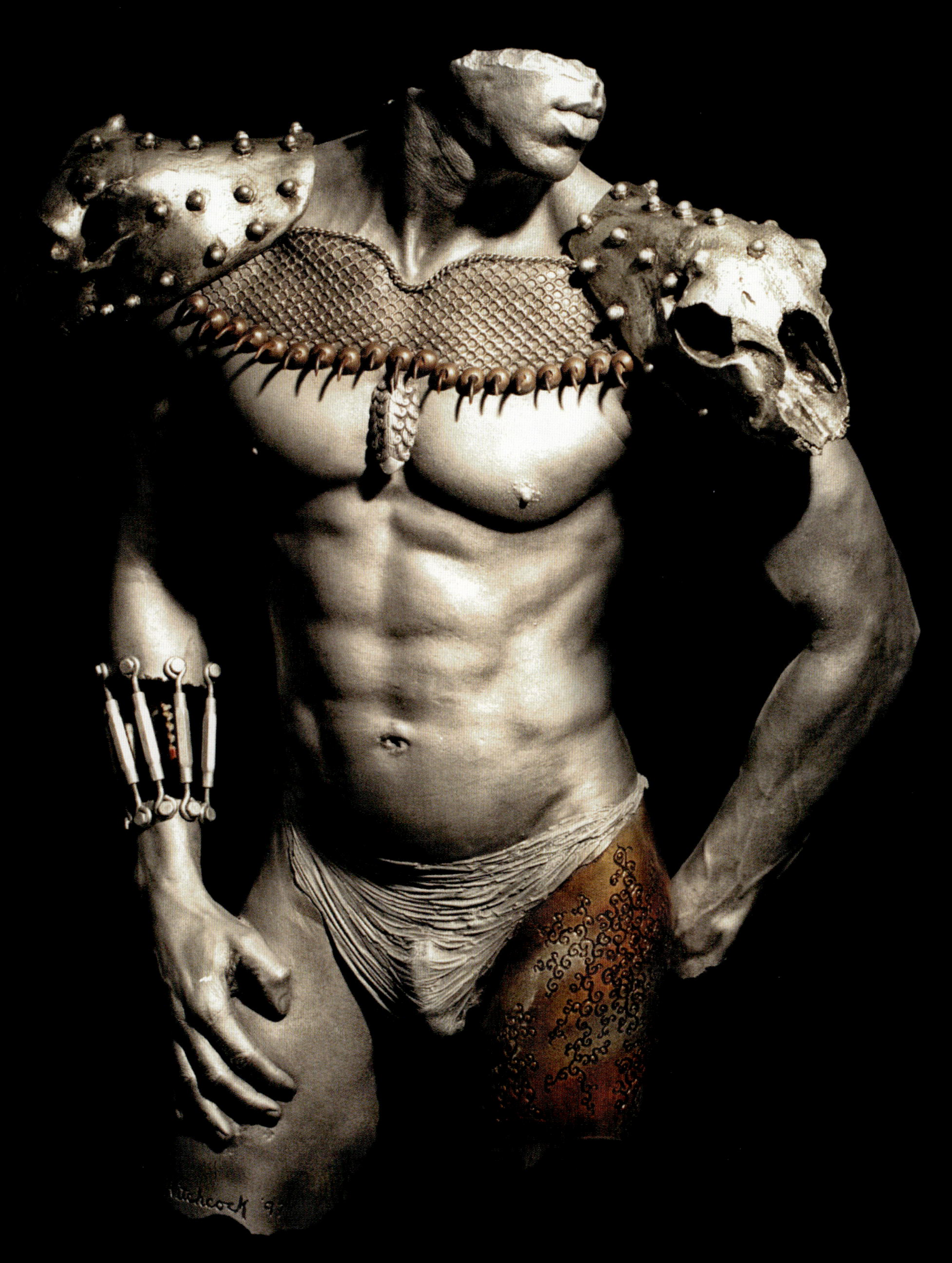

OVERLORD, 1997
cast gypsum, resin, steel, ram horns,
leather, circuit boards
32” x 24” x 14”

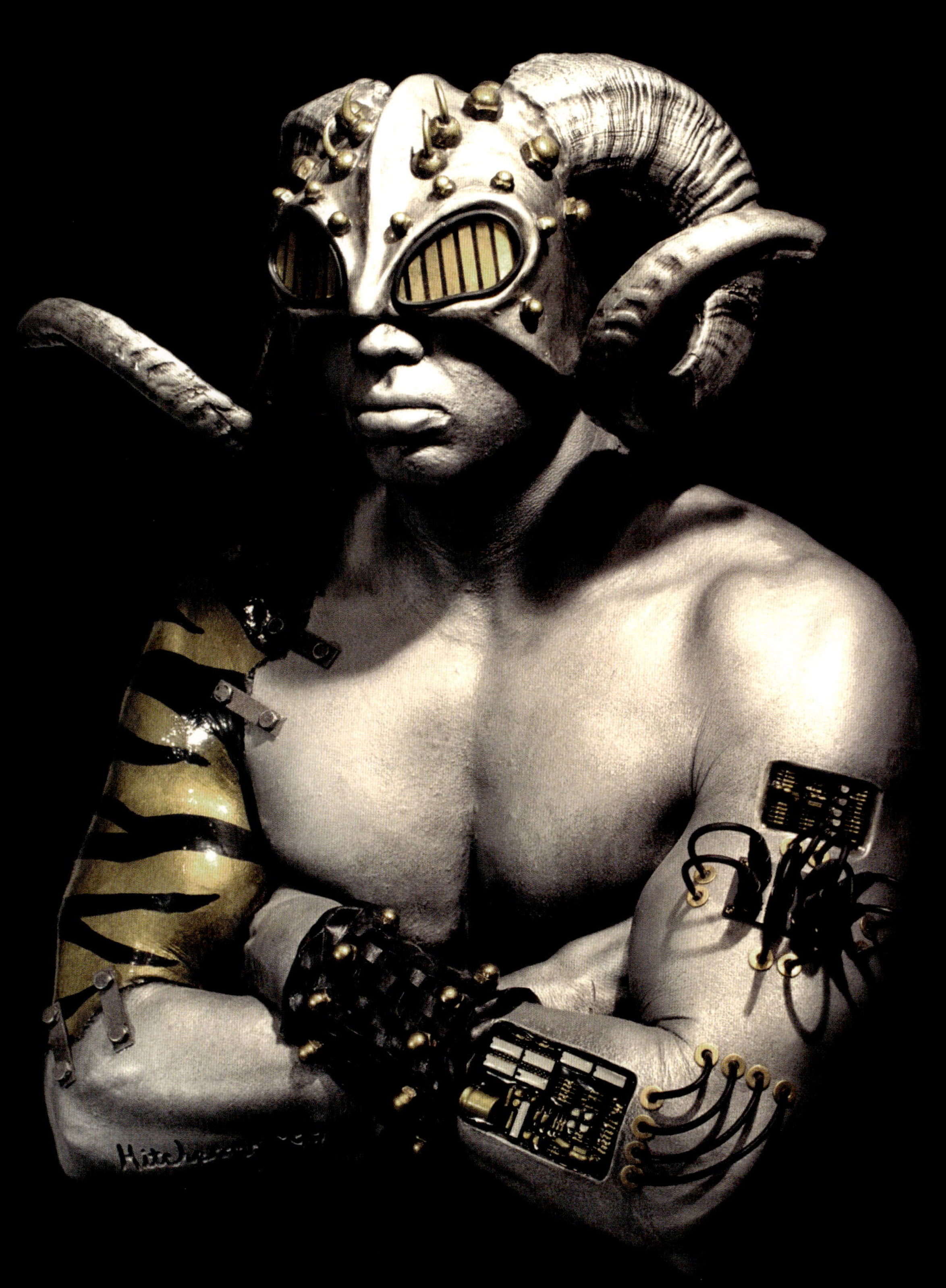

GLADIATOR, 1996
cast gypsum, resin, steel,
28" x 22" x 14"

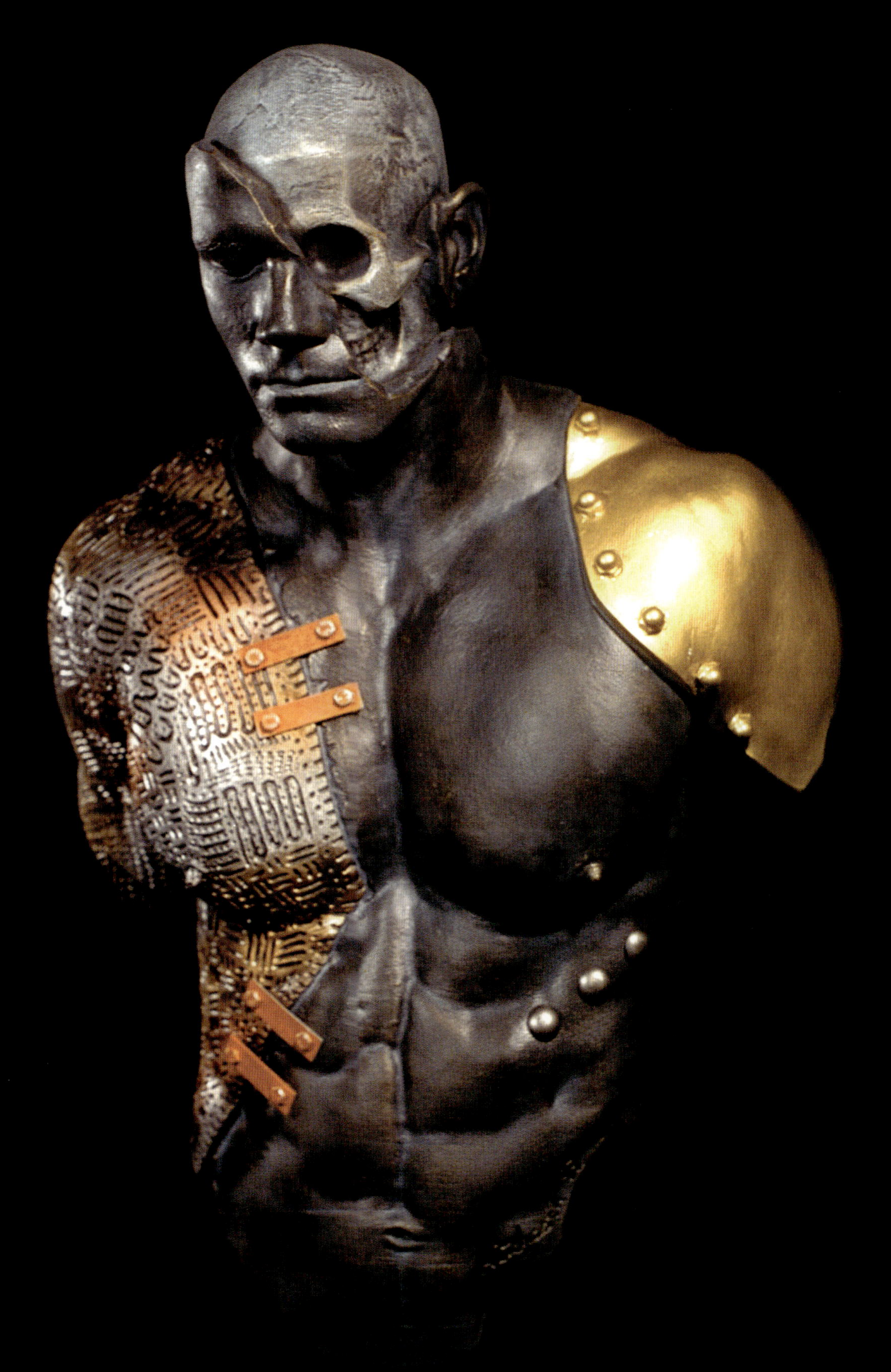

WARRIOR, 1997
cast gypsum, cast resin, acrylic,
muskrat claws, beaver skulls,
32” x 24” x 14”
(inscription reads: “La Fallait est l’illusion de ceux qui ne se concentreat que sur Les Erreurs.”
“Failure is the illusion of those who dwell continuously upon error.”)

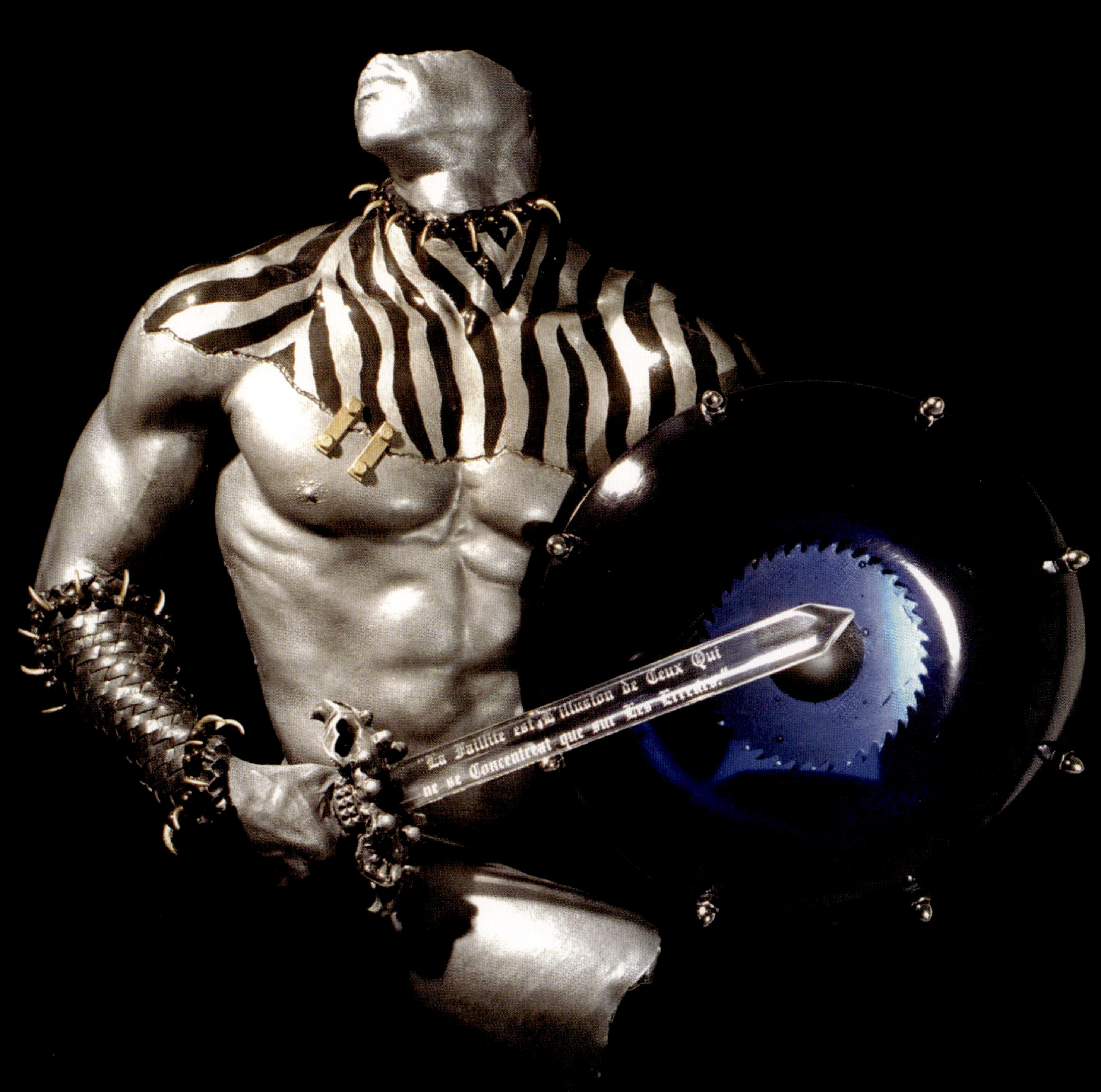
"La Faillite est L'illusion de Ceux Qui
ne se Concentrent que sur Les Erreurs."

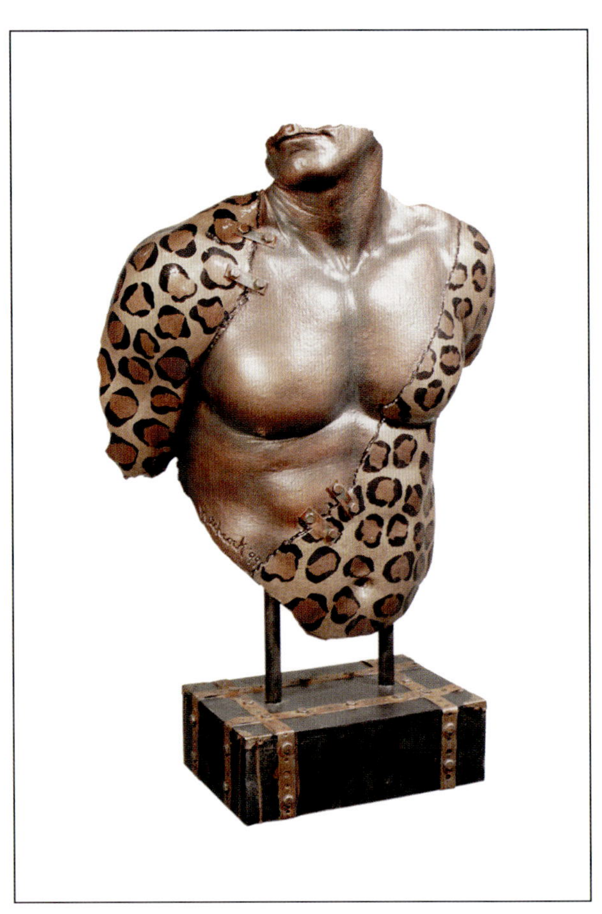

COLOR STUDY FOR WINGED WARRIOR, 1999
cast gypsum, resin, steel,
30" x 20" x 12" *Model: James Hayes*
WINGED WARRIOR, 1999 *(right)*
cast gypsum, steel, fiberglass, bone,
78" x 48" x 16"

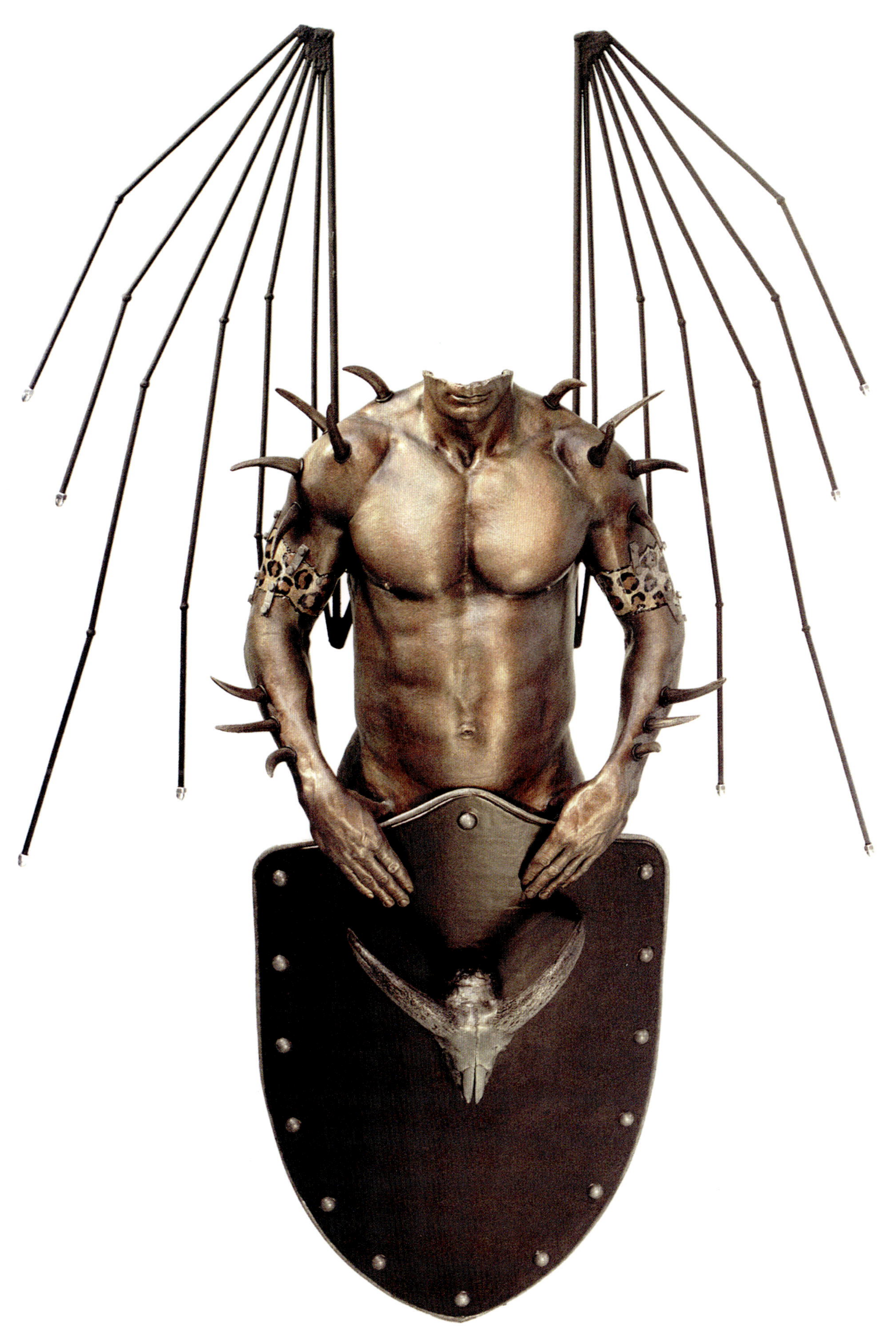

SENTRY, 1998
cast gypsum, resin, steel,
42" x 24" x 14"

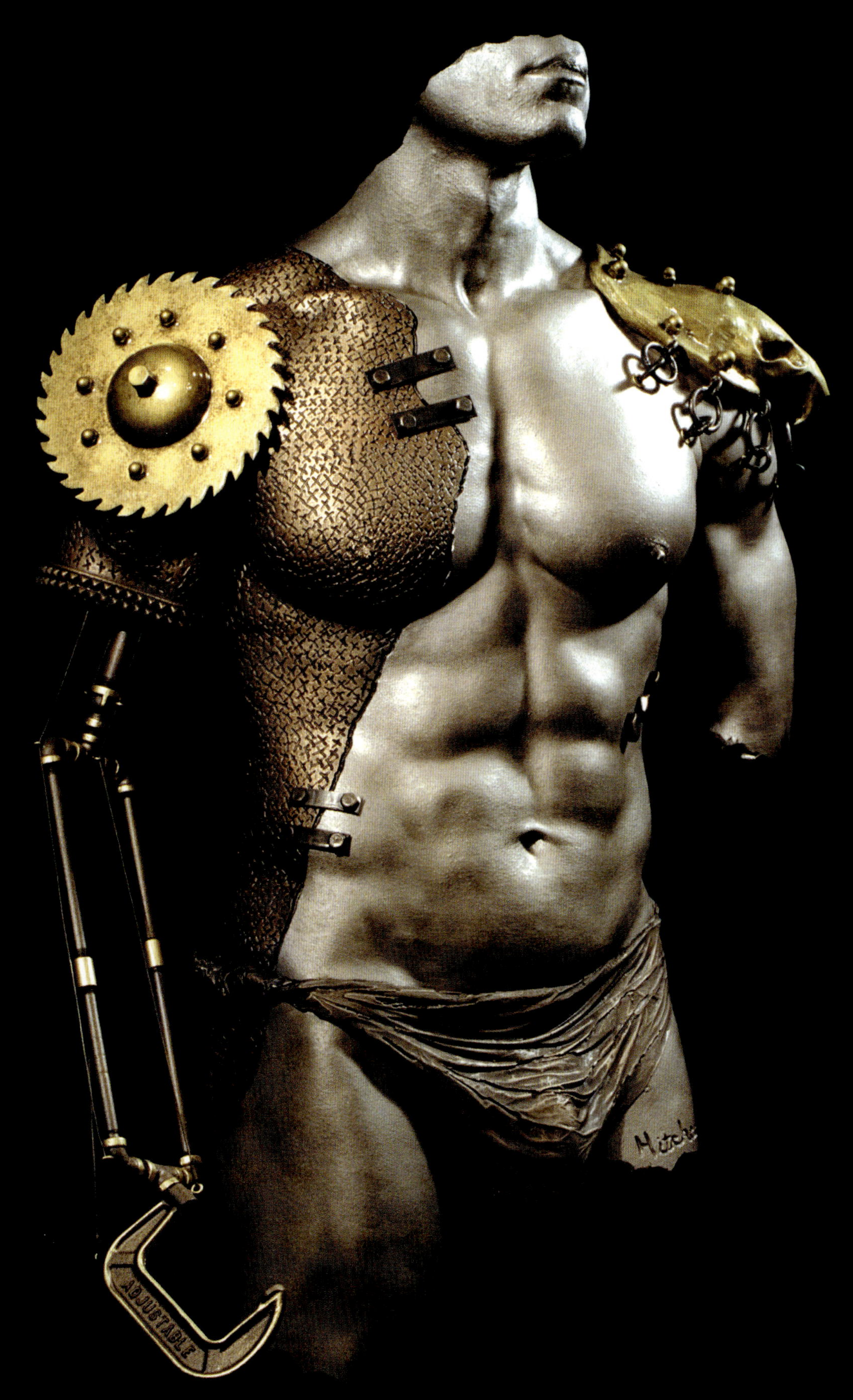
ADJUSTABLE

MERCURY, 1998
cast gypsum, resin, steel, copper,
24” x 20” x 12”

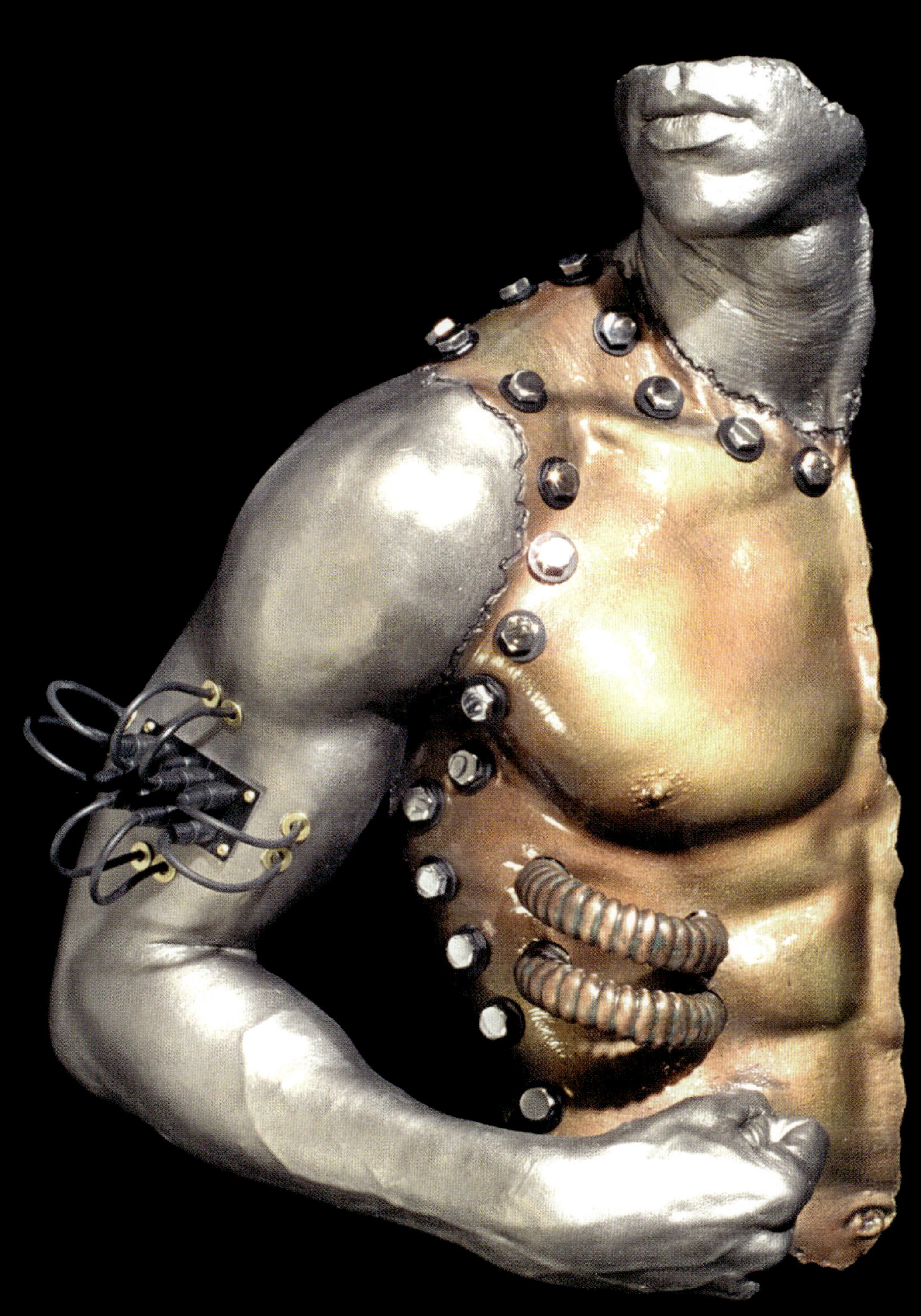

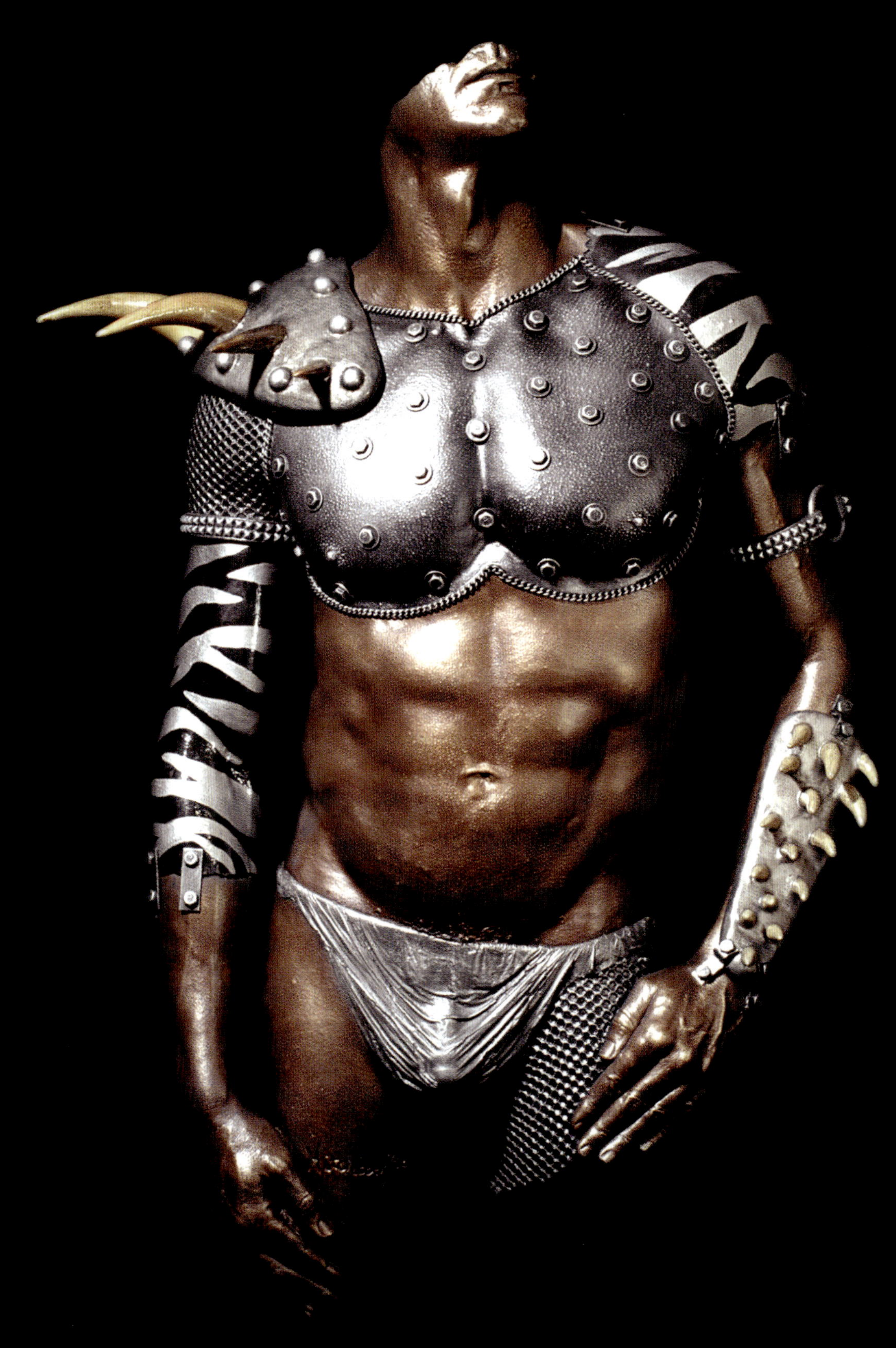

PRISONER, 1998
cast gypsum, resin, steel, rope, horn,
42" x 26" x 18"
(right) **BISHOP, 1999**
cast gypsum, resin, steel,
72" x 28" x 16"

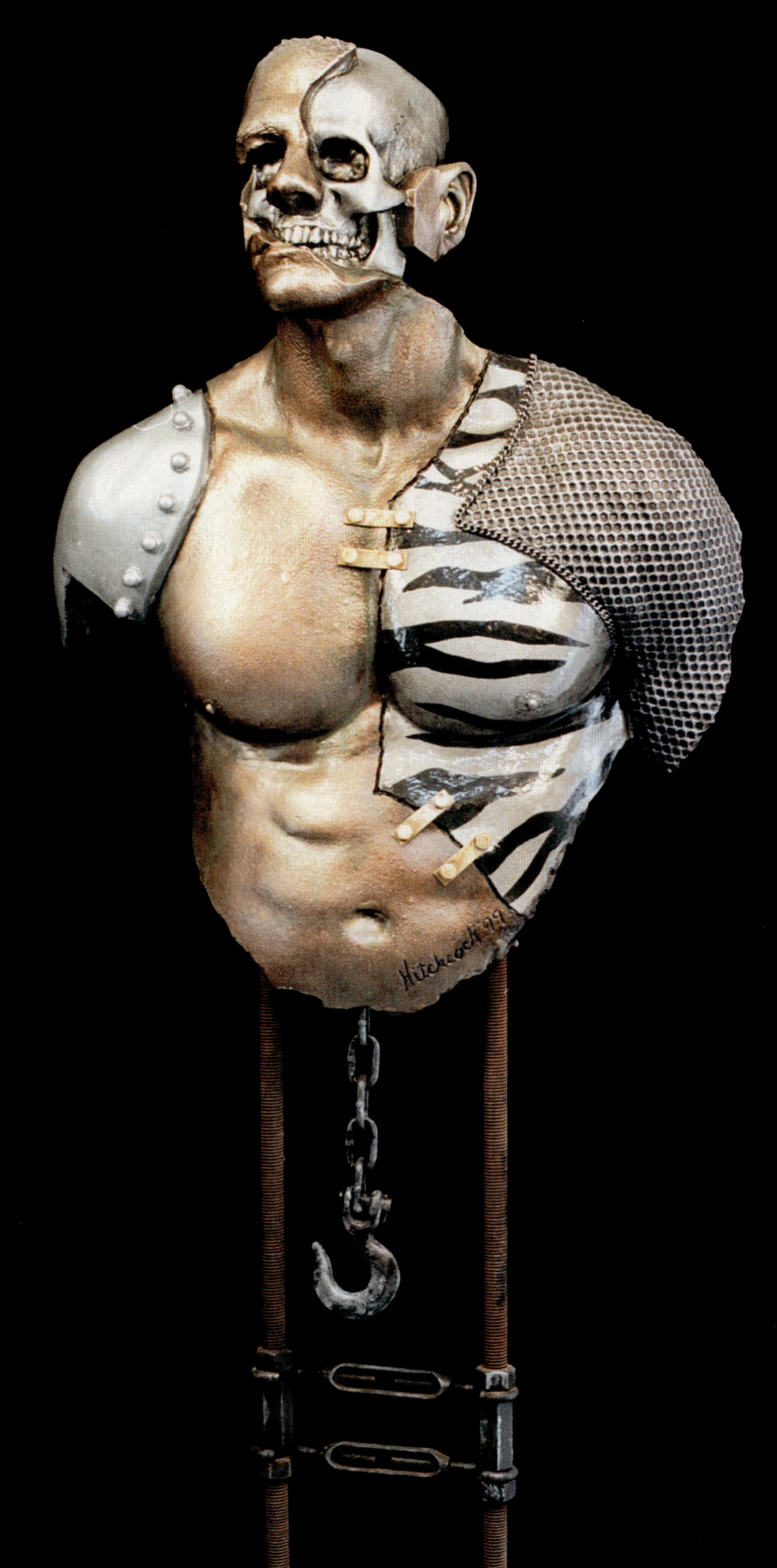
Hitchcock '99

HERO'S WELCOME, 1998
cast gypsum, resin, steel, bovine teeth, mink skulls,
42" x 24" x 14"

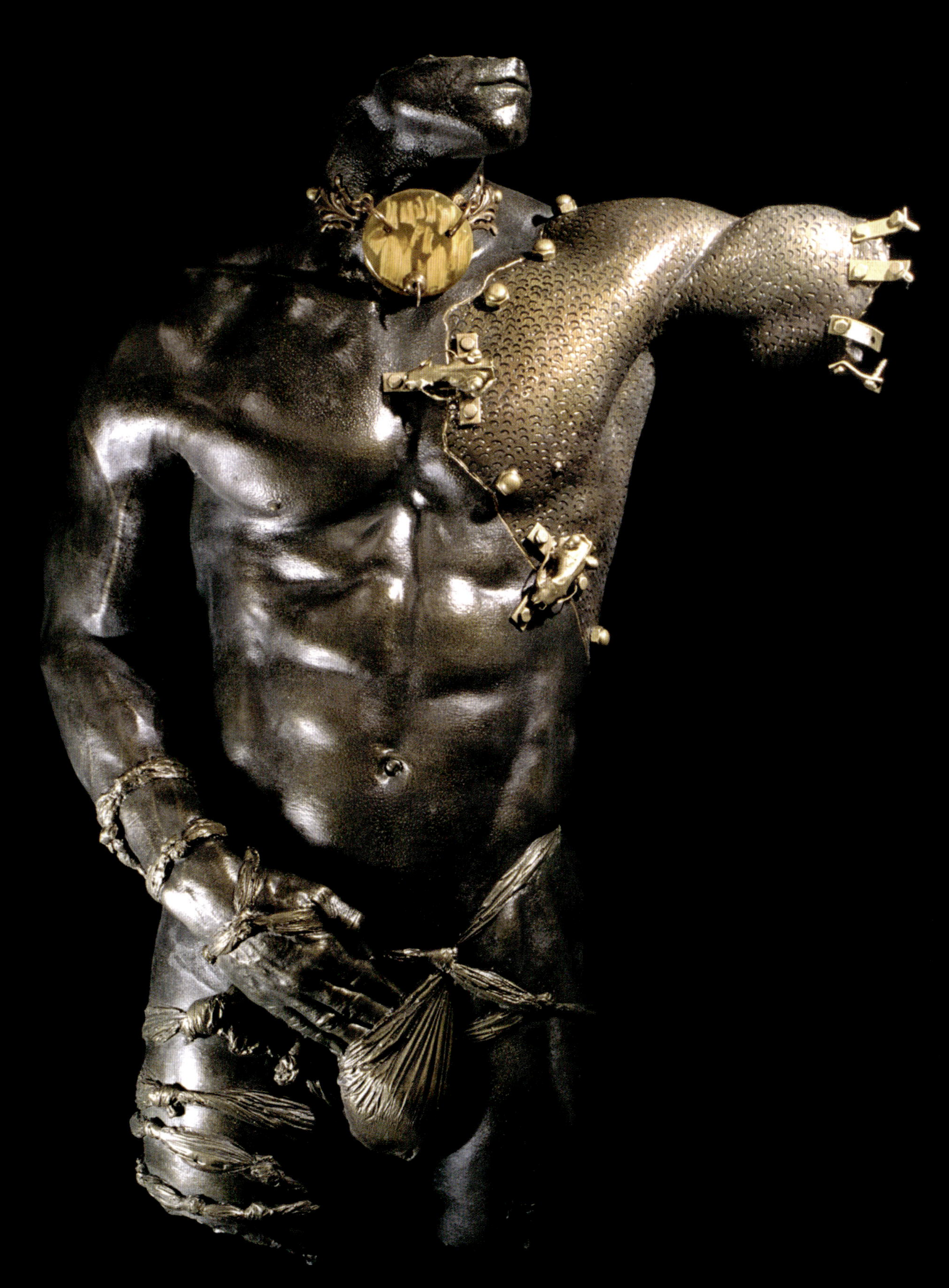

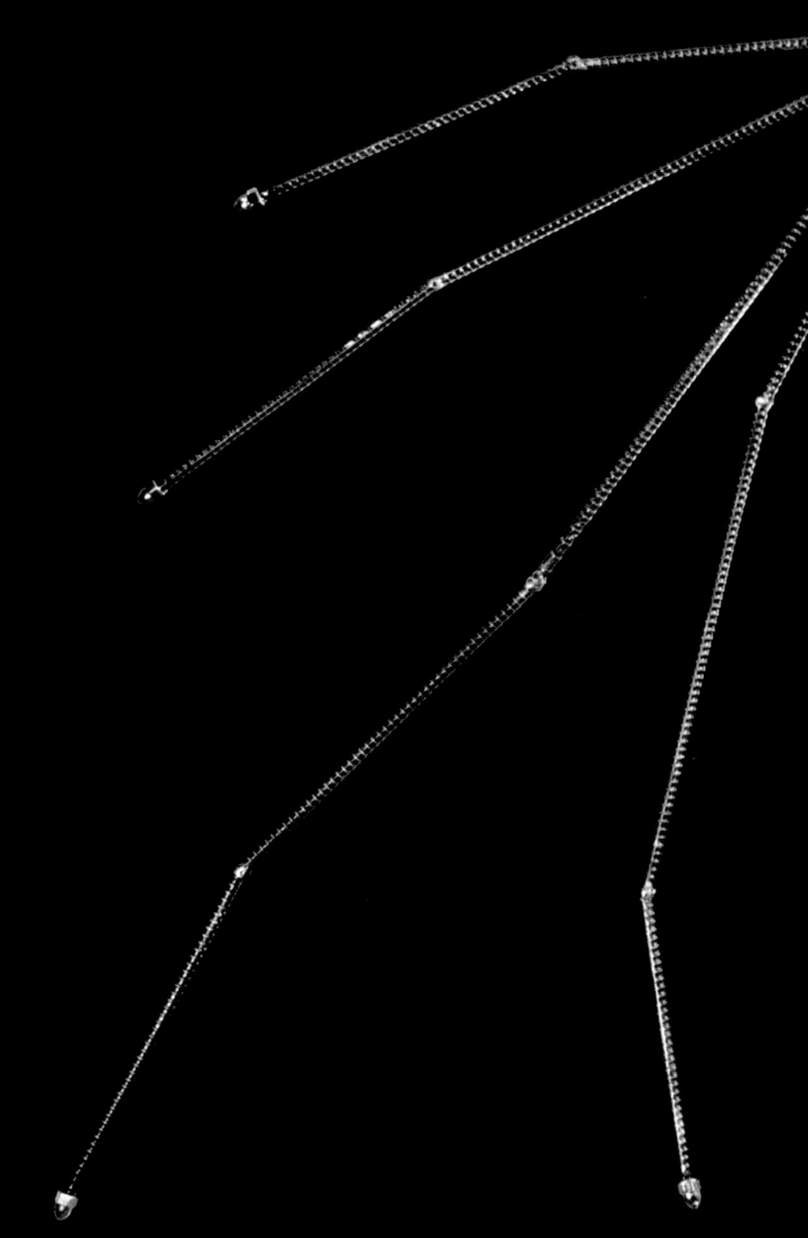

FALLEN ANGEL, 1998
cast gypsum, rebar, horn,
42" x 84" x 18"

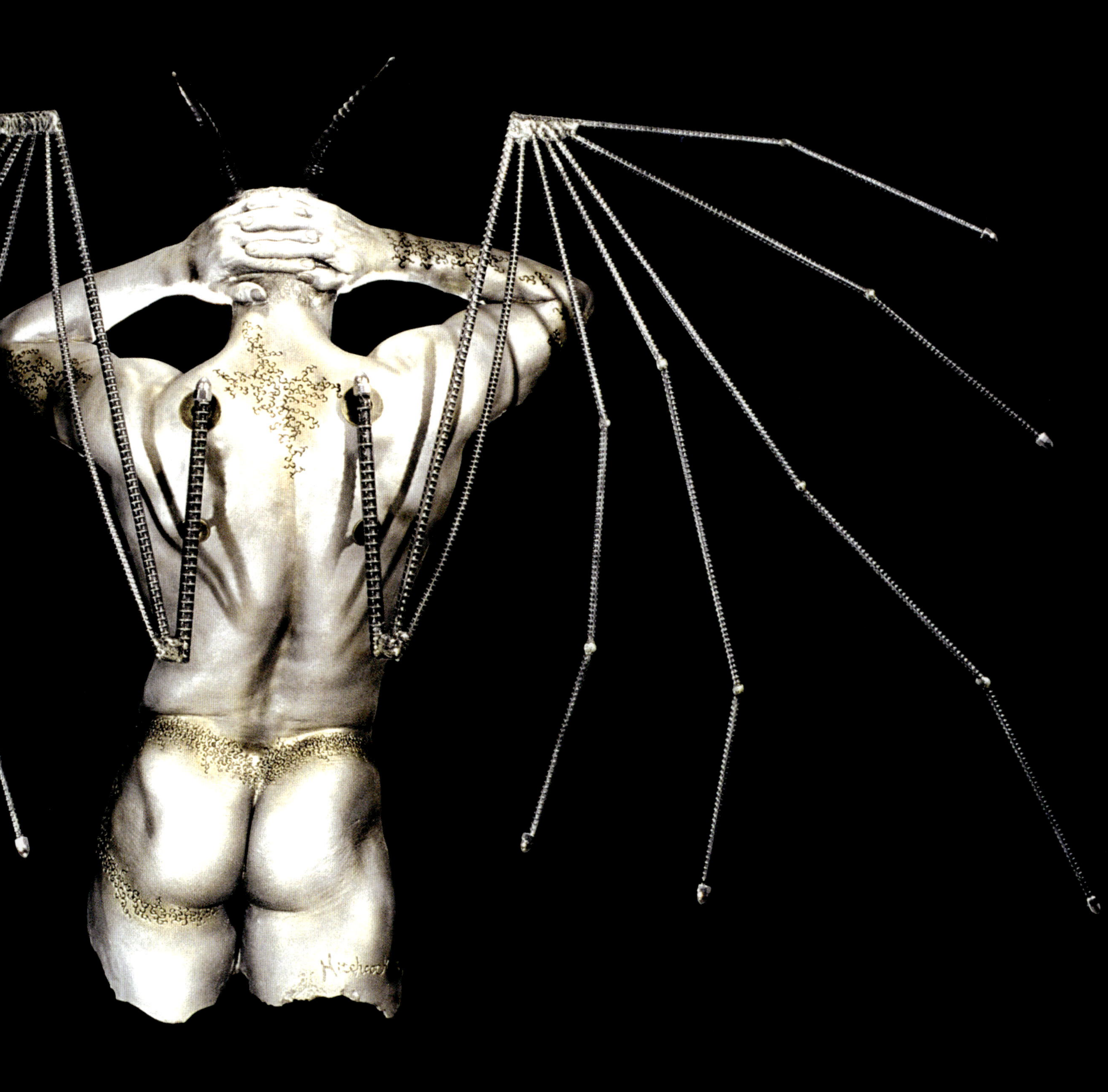

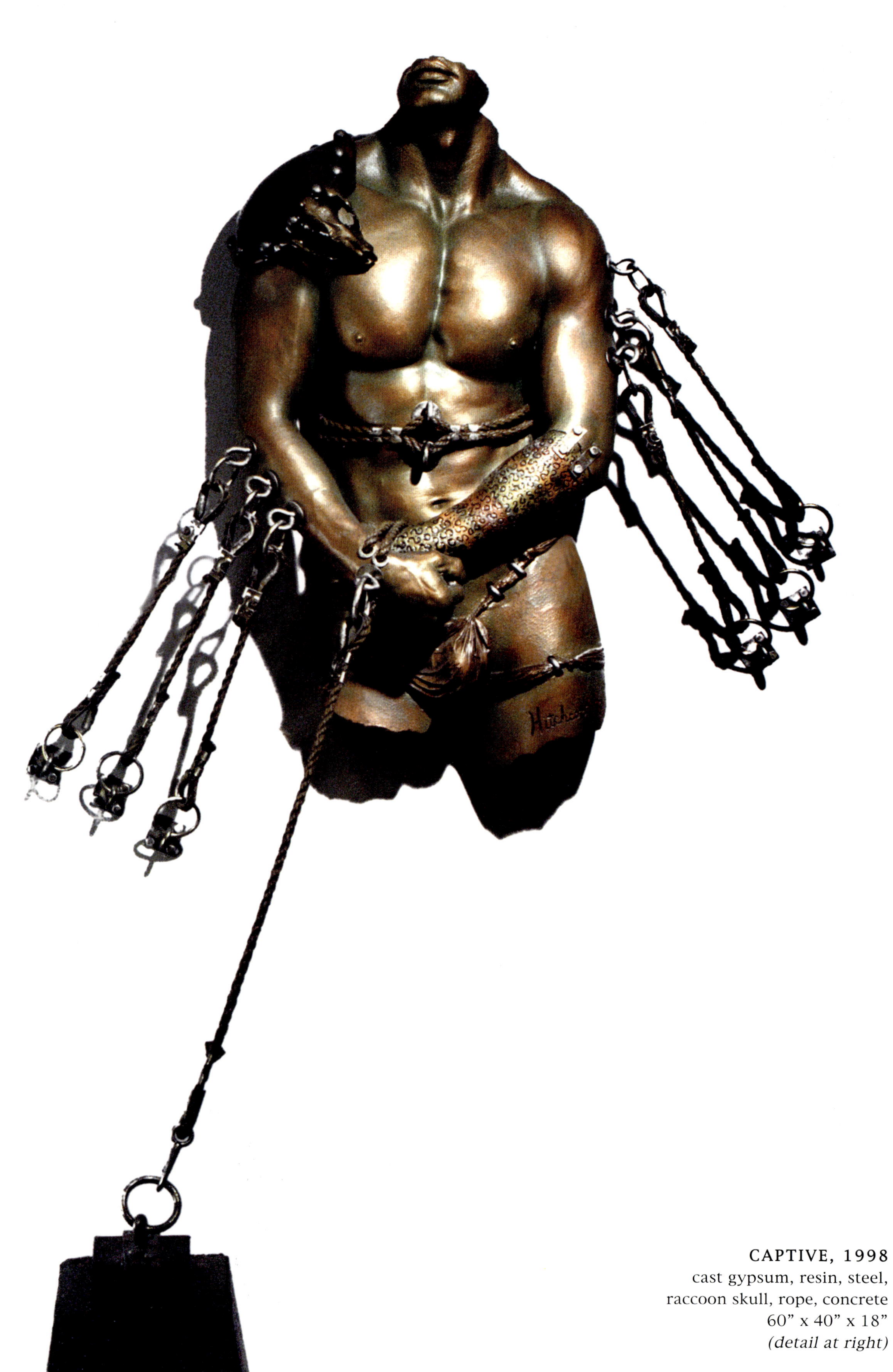

CAPTIVE, 1998
cast gypsum, resin, steel,
raccoon skull, rope, concrete
60” x 40” x 18”
(detail at right)

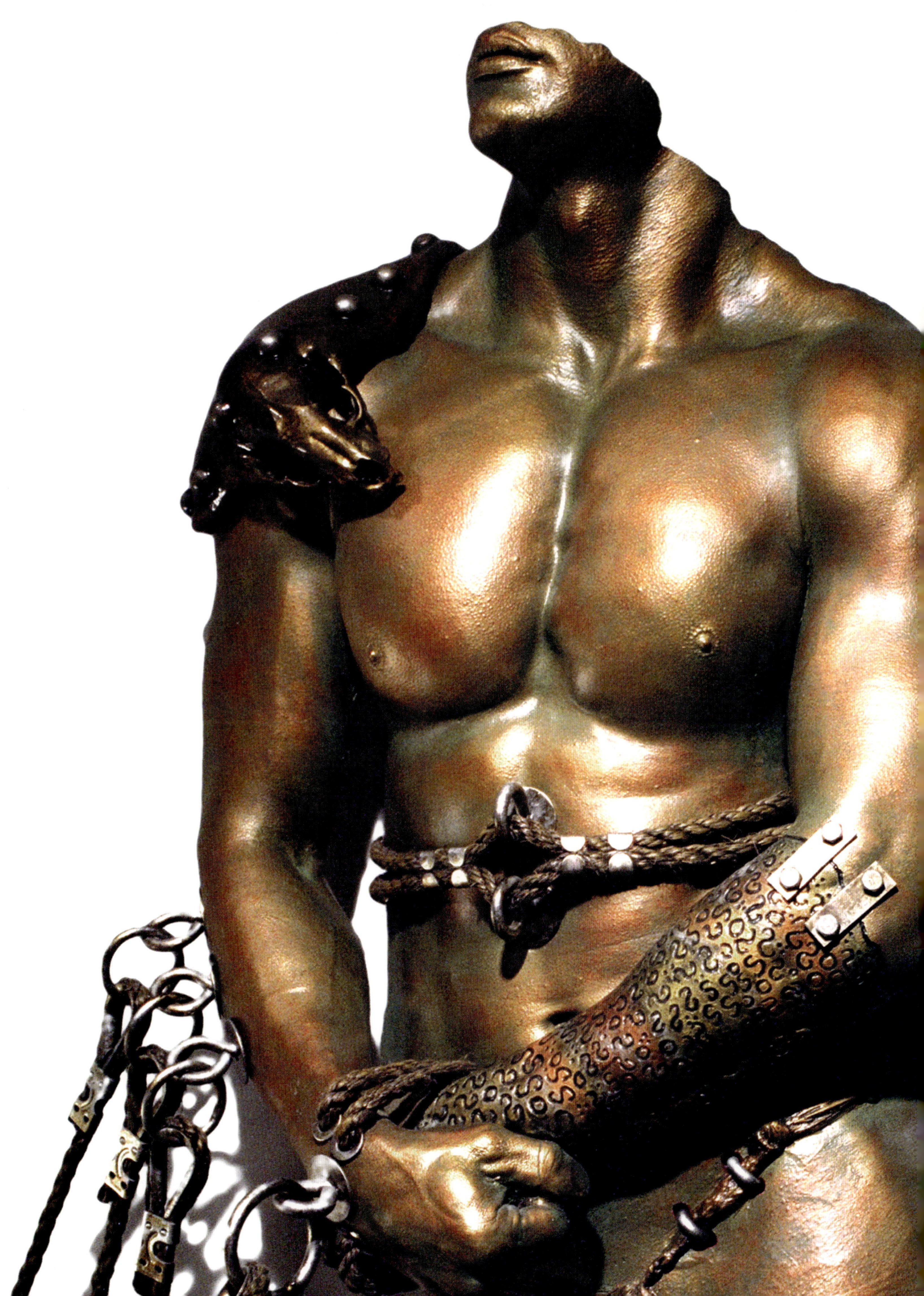

THE CHOSEN, 1997
cast gypsum, fiberglass, cast resin,
72” x 72” x 18”

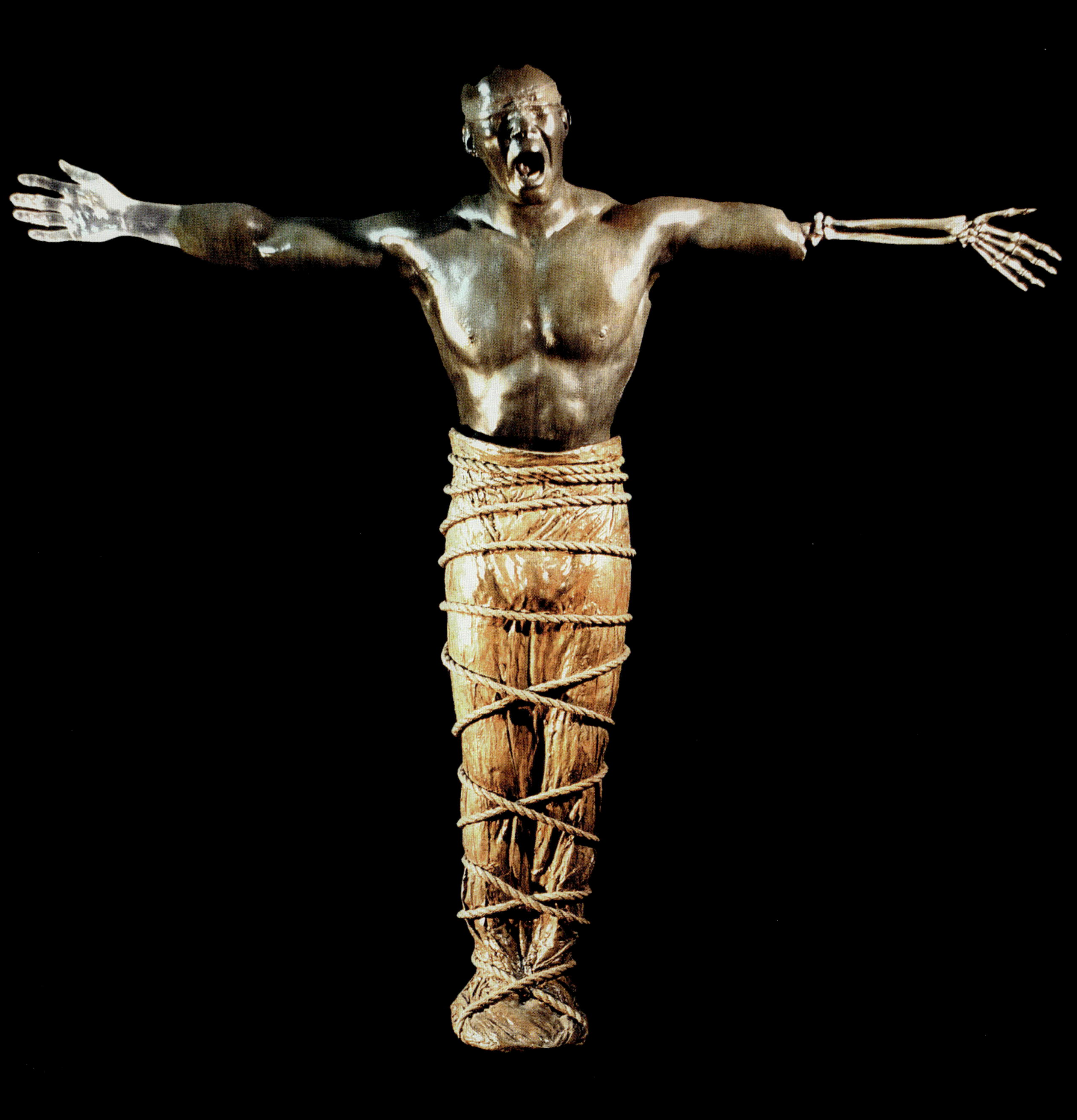

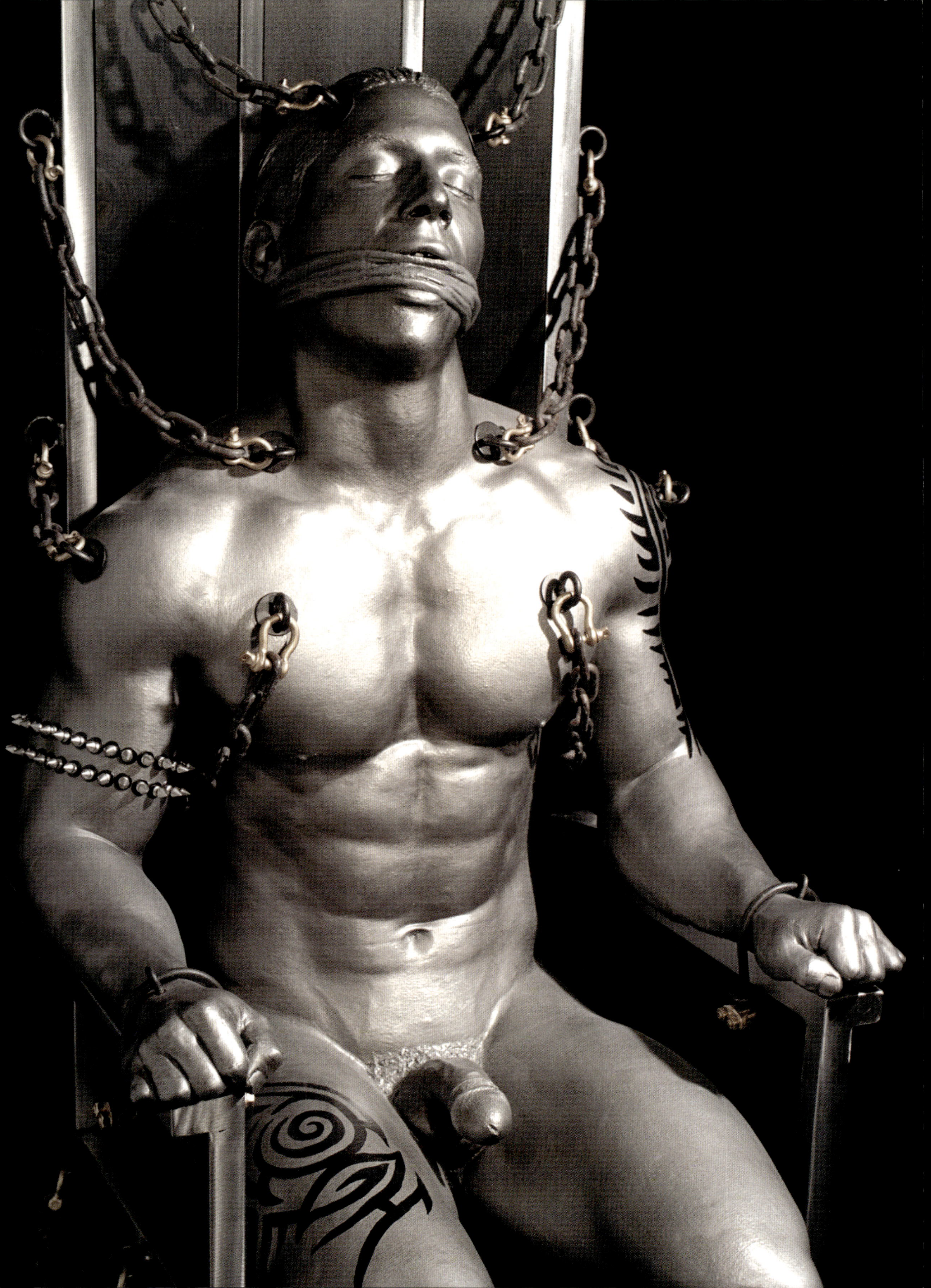

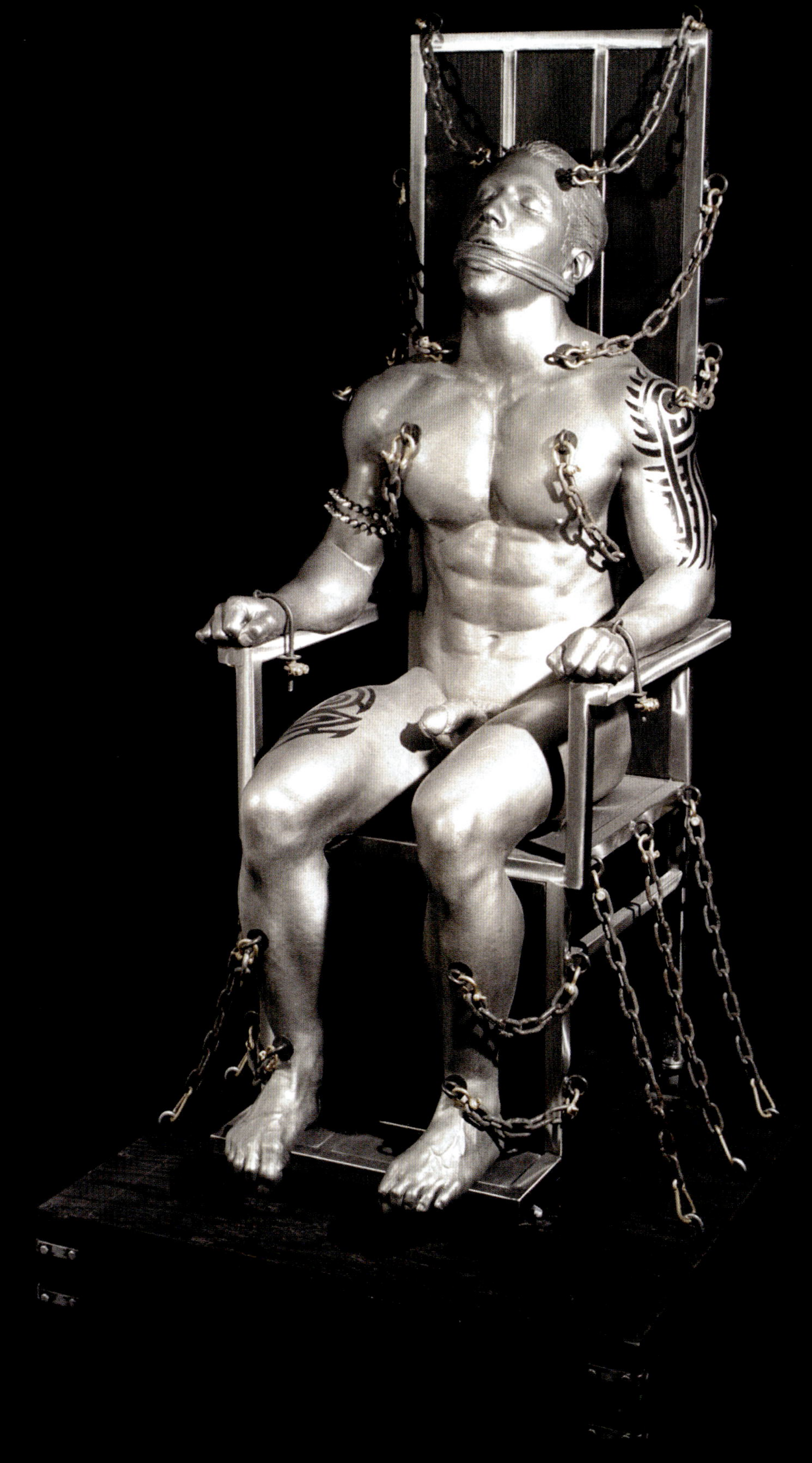

SEATED MALE, 1999
cast gypsum, steel, wood,
60" x 30" x 30"
(detail at left)

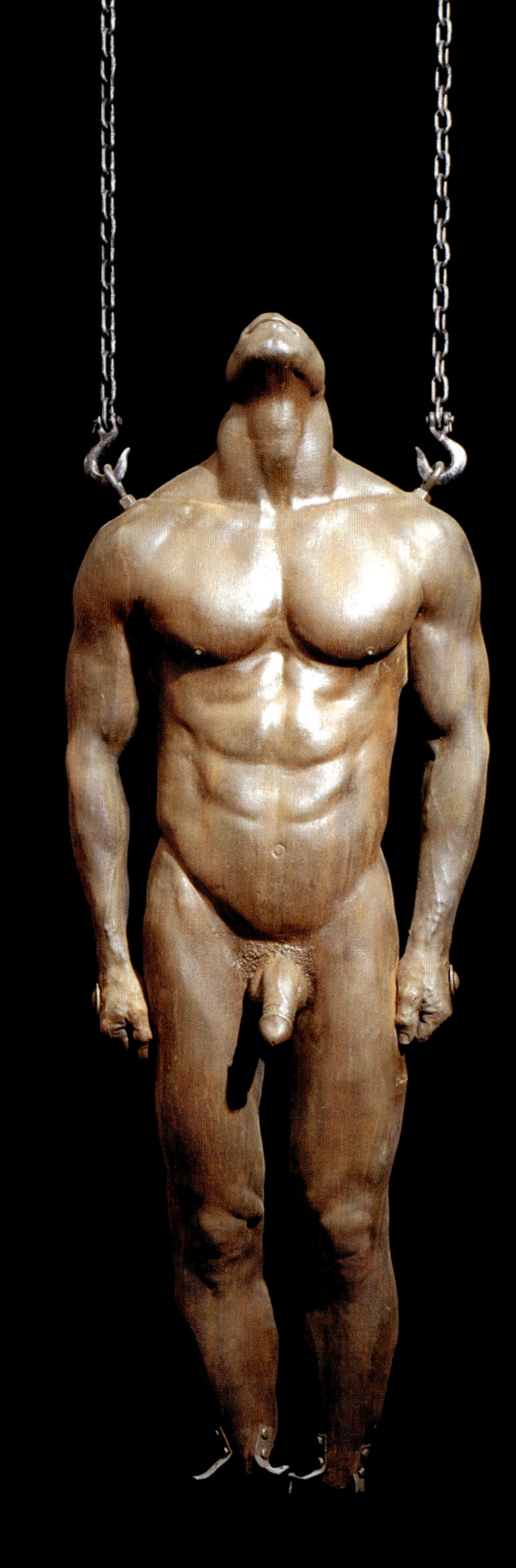

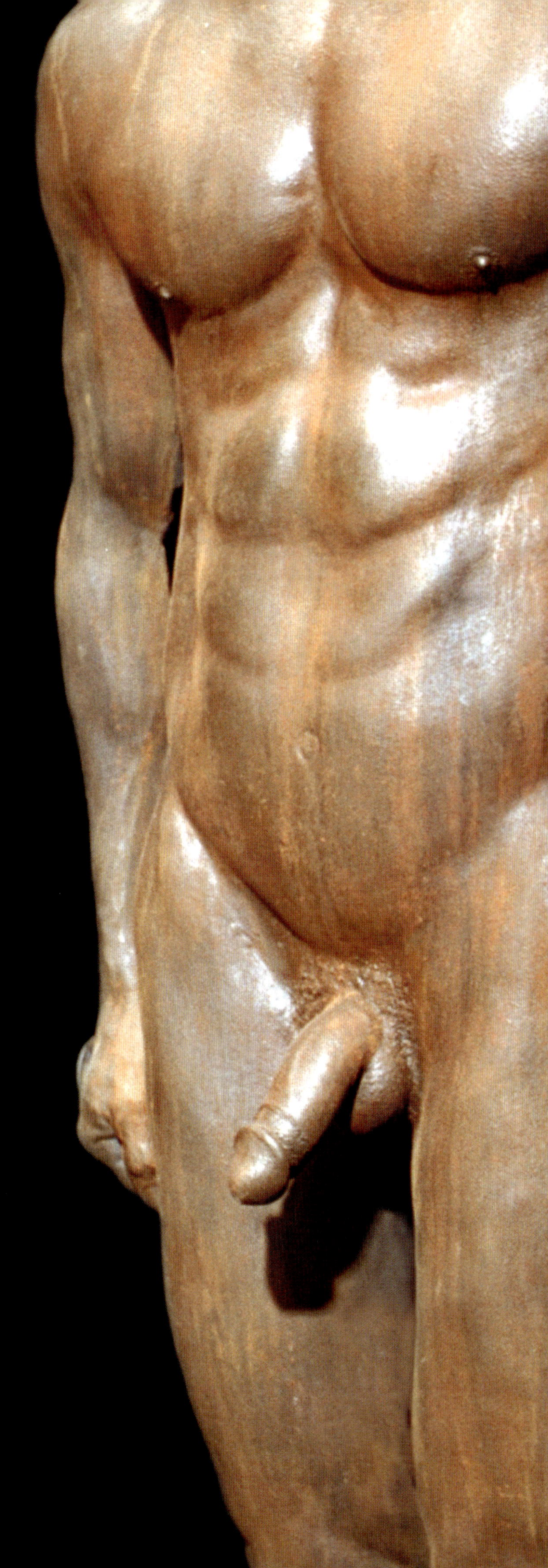

KOUROS '98, 1998
cast gypsum, steel,
66" x 24" x 14" on 22' chains
(detail at right)

MASON, 1996
cast gypsum,
42” x 26” x 14”

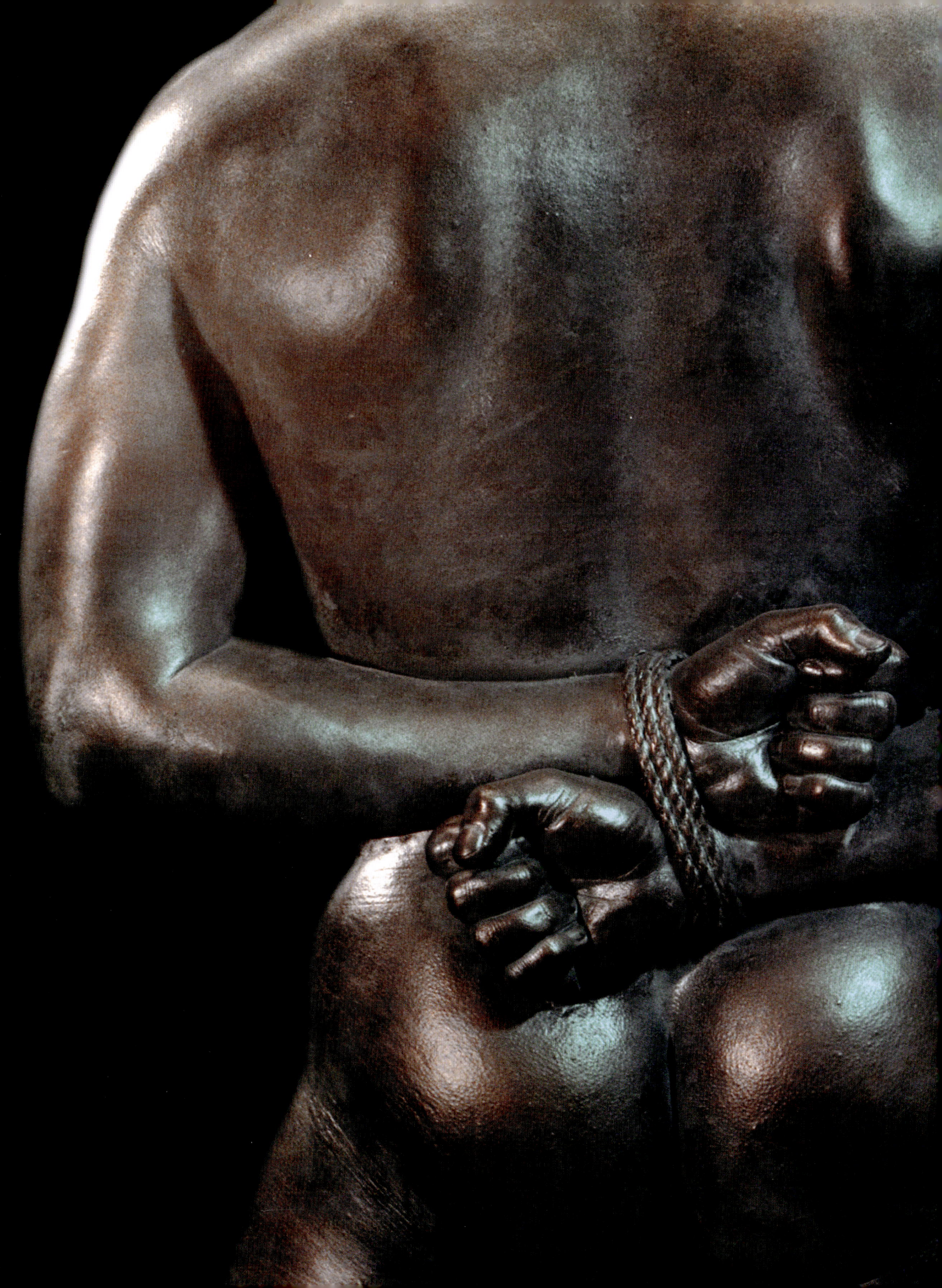

ECSTASY BOUND, 1999
cast gypsum, rope, steel,
66" x 26" x 14"

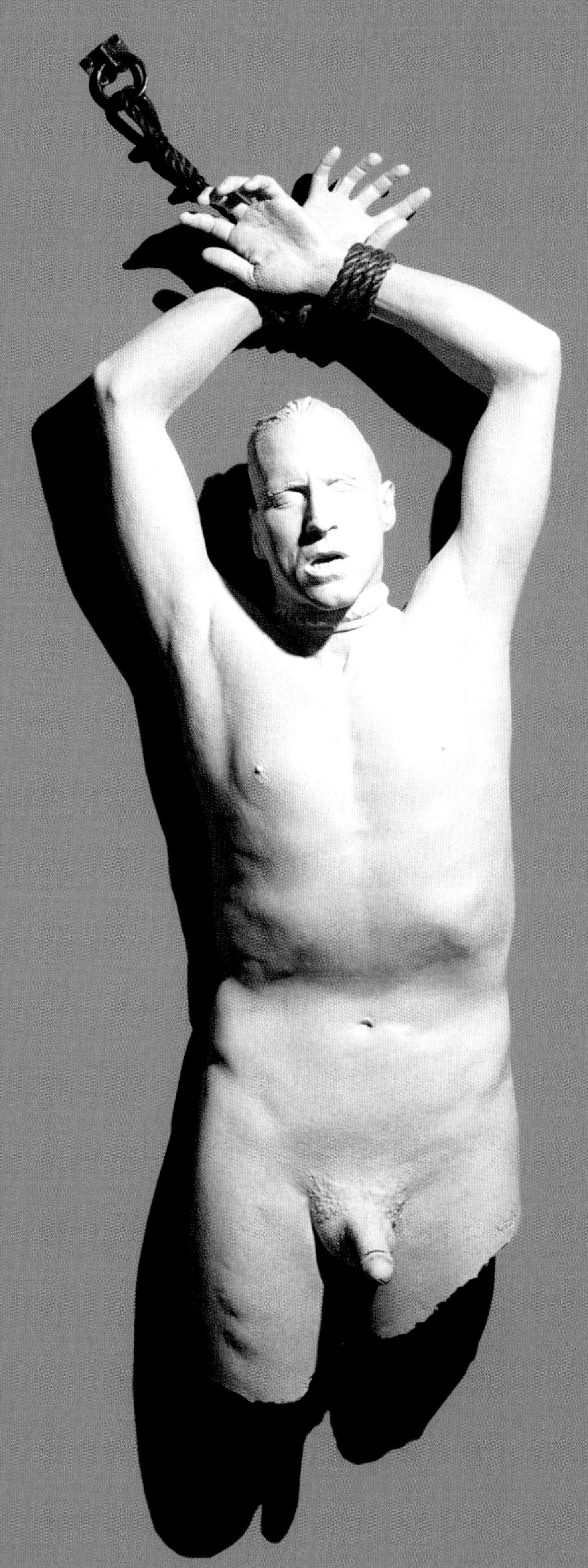

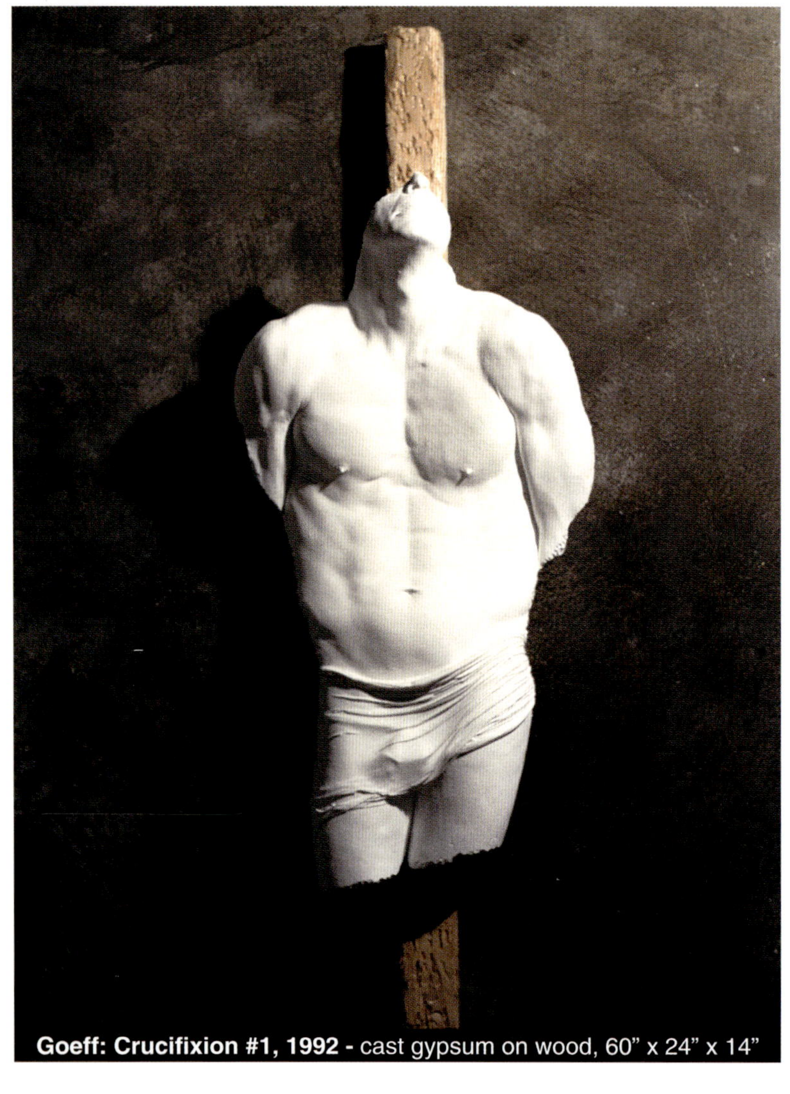
Goeff: Crucifixion #1, 1992 - cast gypsum on wood, 60” x 24” x 14”

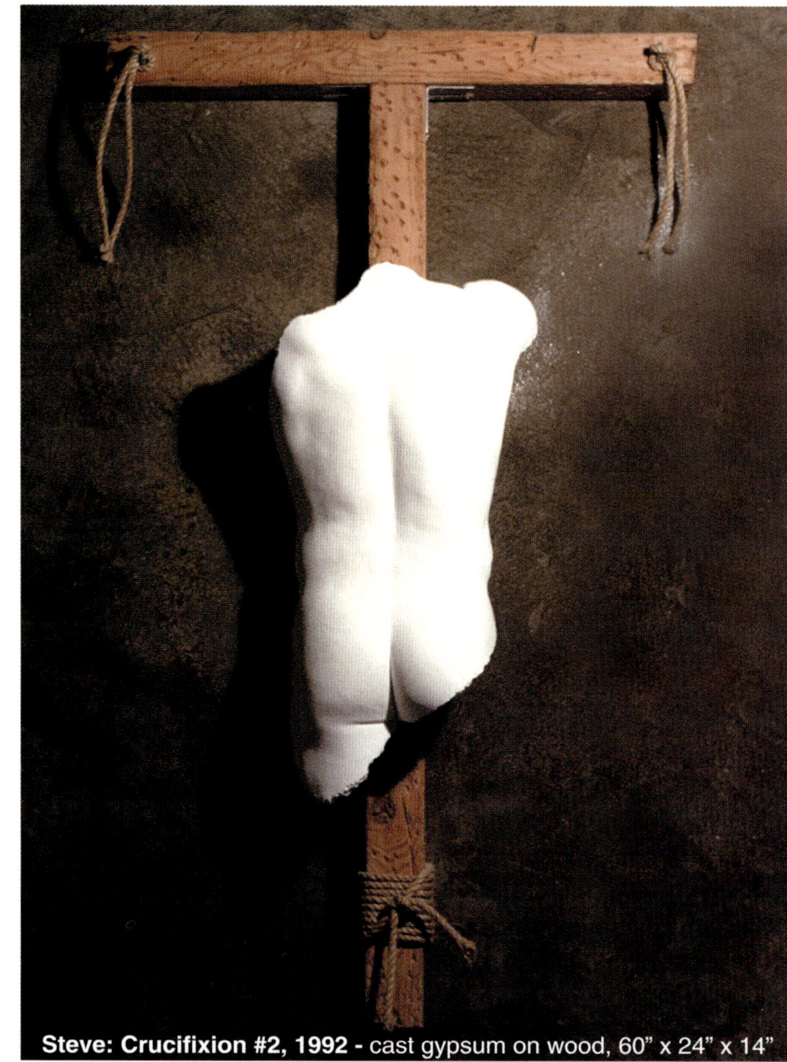
Steve: Crucifixion #2, 1992 - cast gypsum on wood, 60” x 24” x 14”

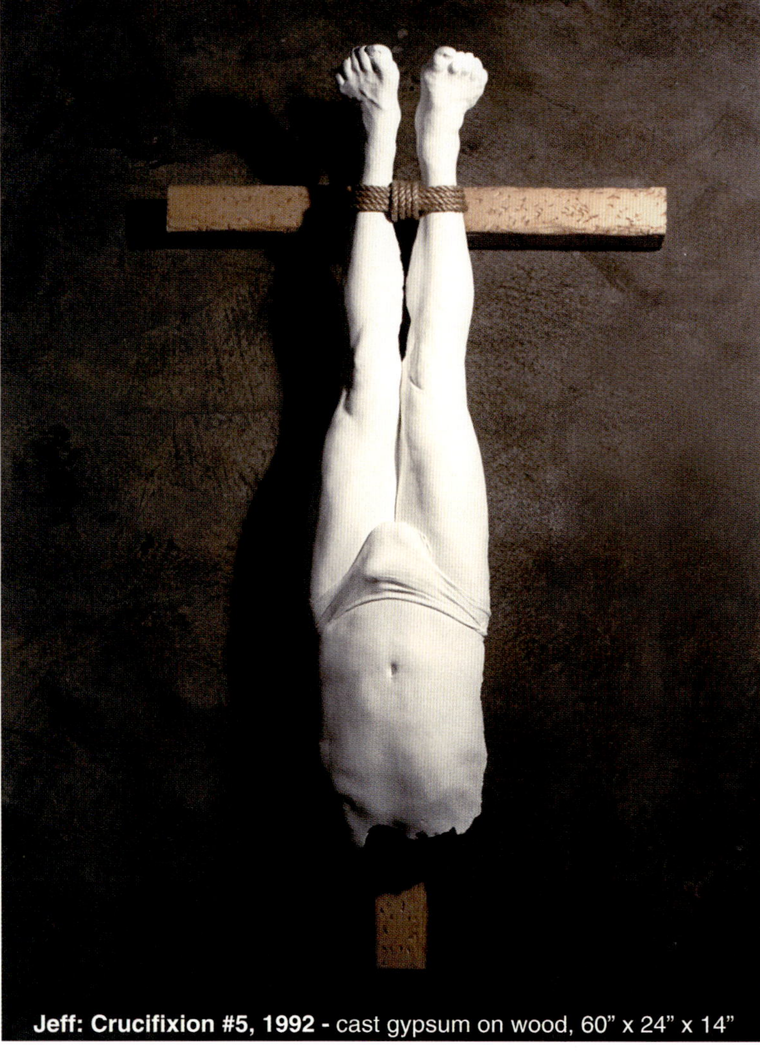
Jeff: Crucifixion #5, 1992 - cast gypsum on wood, 60” x 24” x 14”

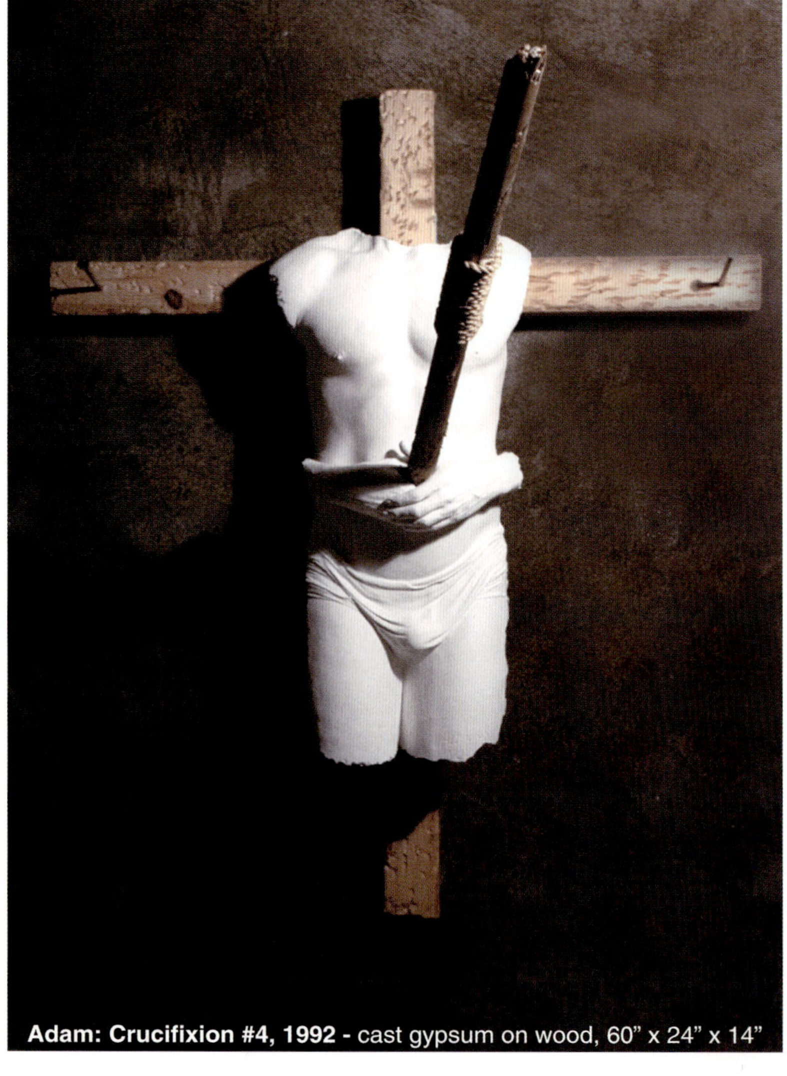
Adam: Crucifixion #4, 1992 - cast gypsum on wood, 60” x 24” x 14”

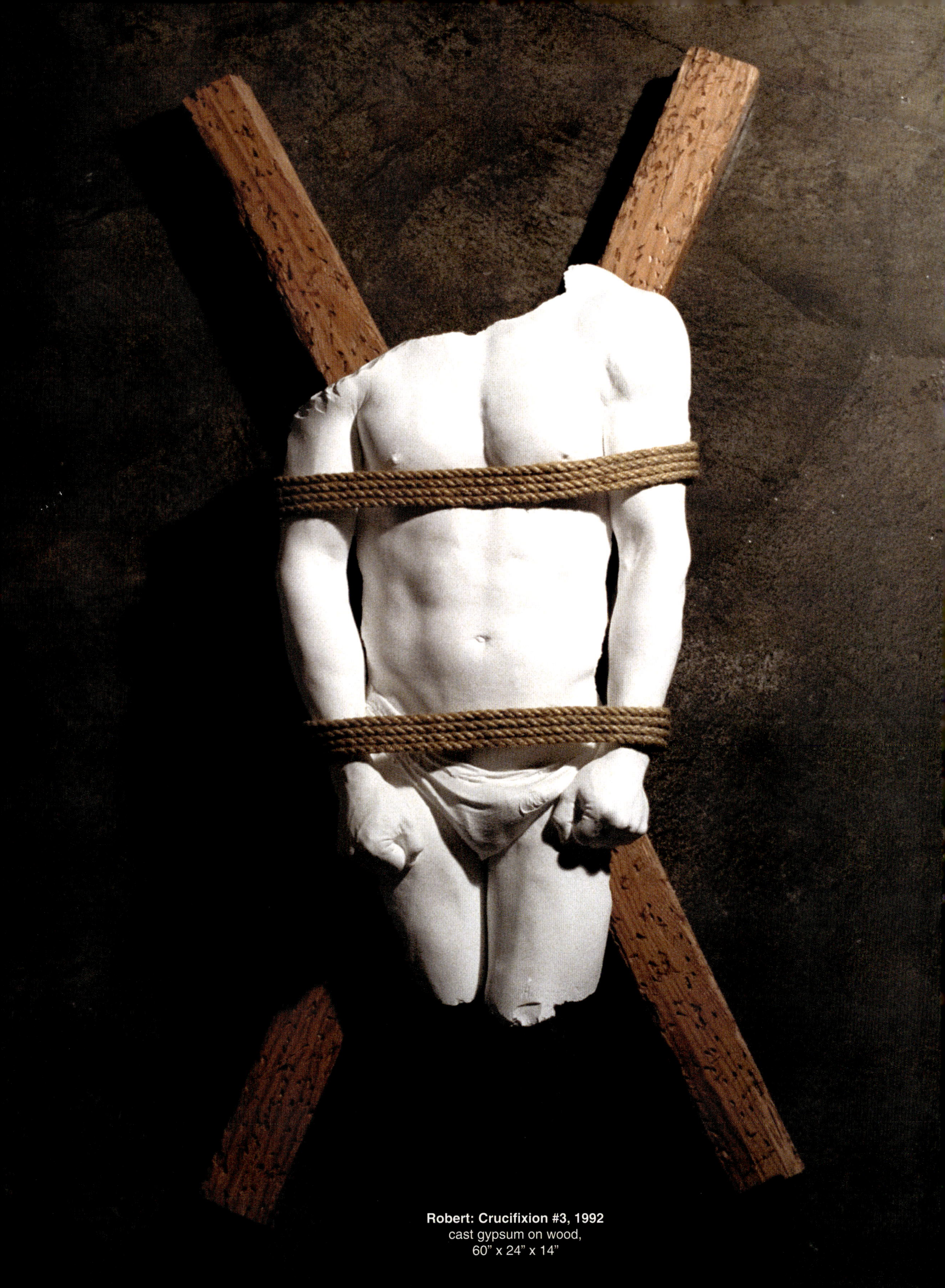

Robert: Crucifixion #3, 1992
cast gypsum on wood,
60" x 24" x 14"

SEBASTIAN, 1998
cast gypsum, wood, steel,
60" x 24" x 14"

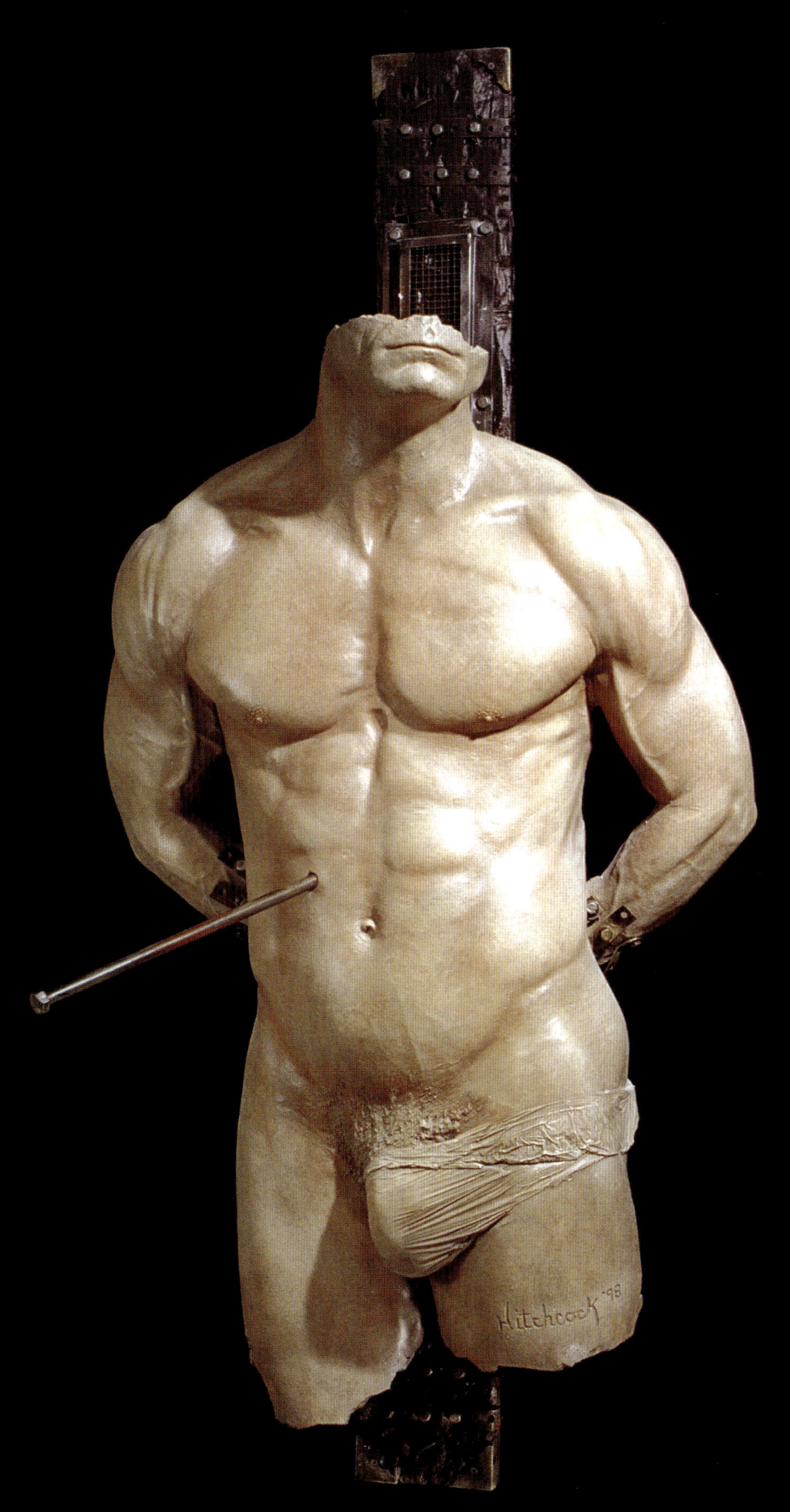
Hitchcock '98

SHEPHERD, 1998
cast gypsum, steel,
90” x 24” x 18” *Model: Tim Smith*

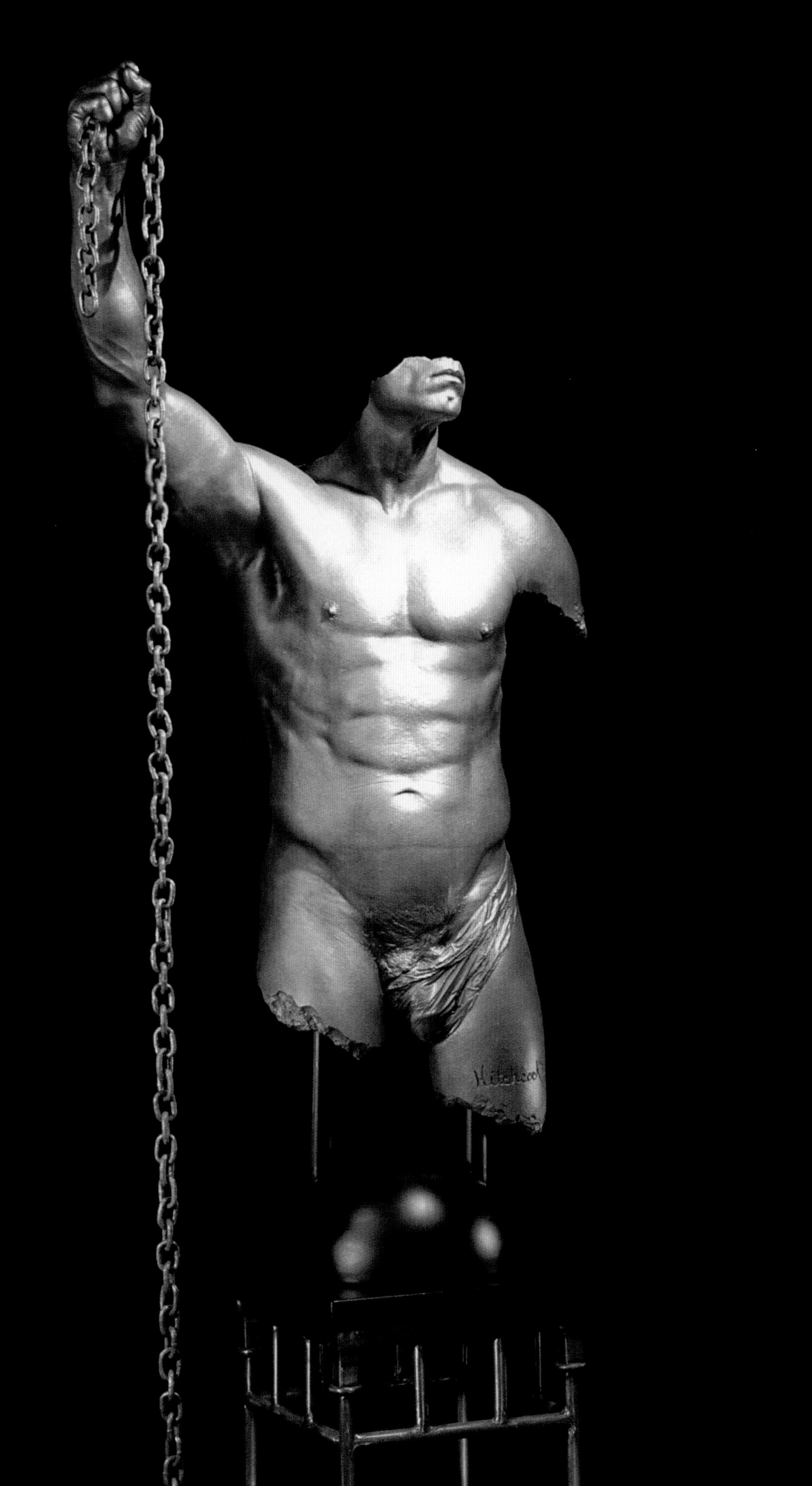

FREEDOM, 1996
cast gypsum, steel,
36" x 48" x 14"

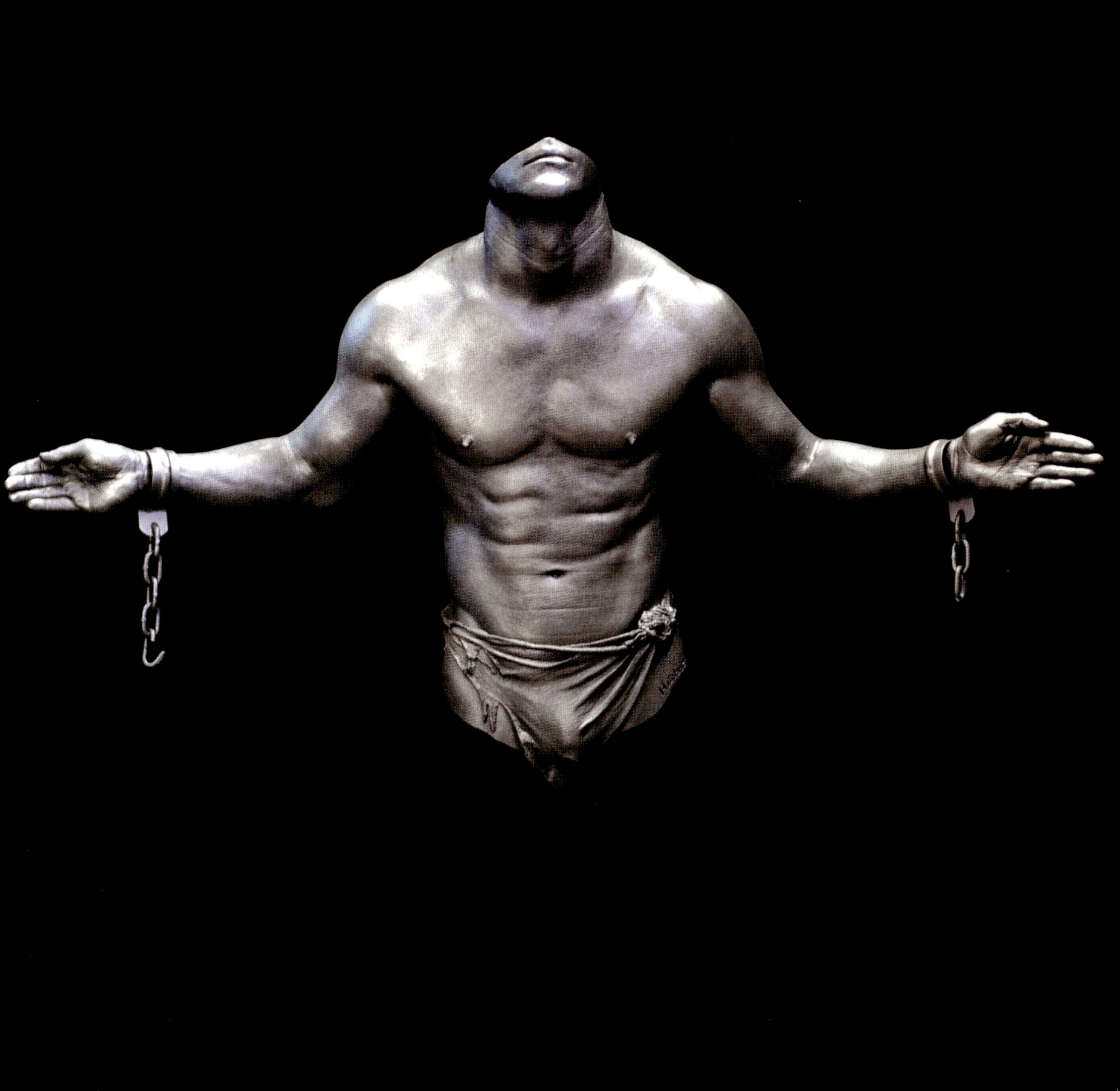

DYING SLAVES, 1998
cast gypsum,
48" x 24" x 14" each

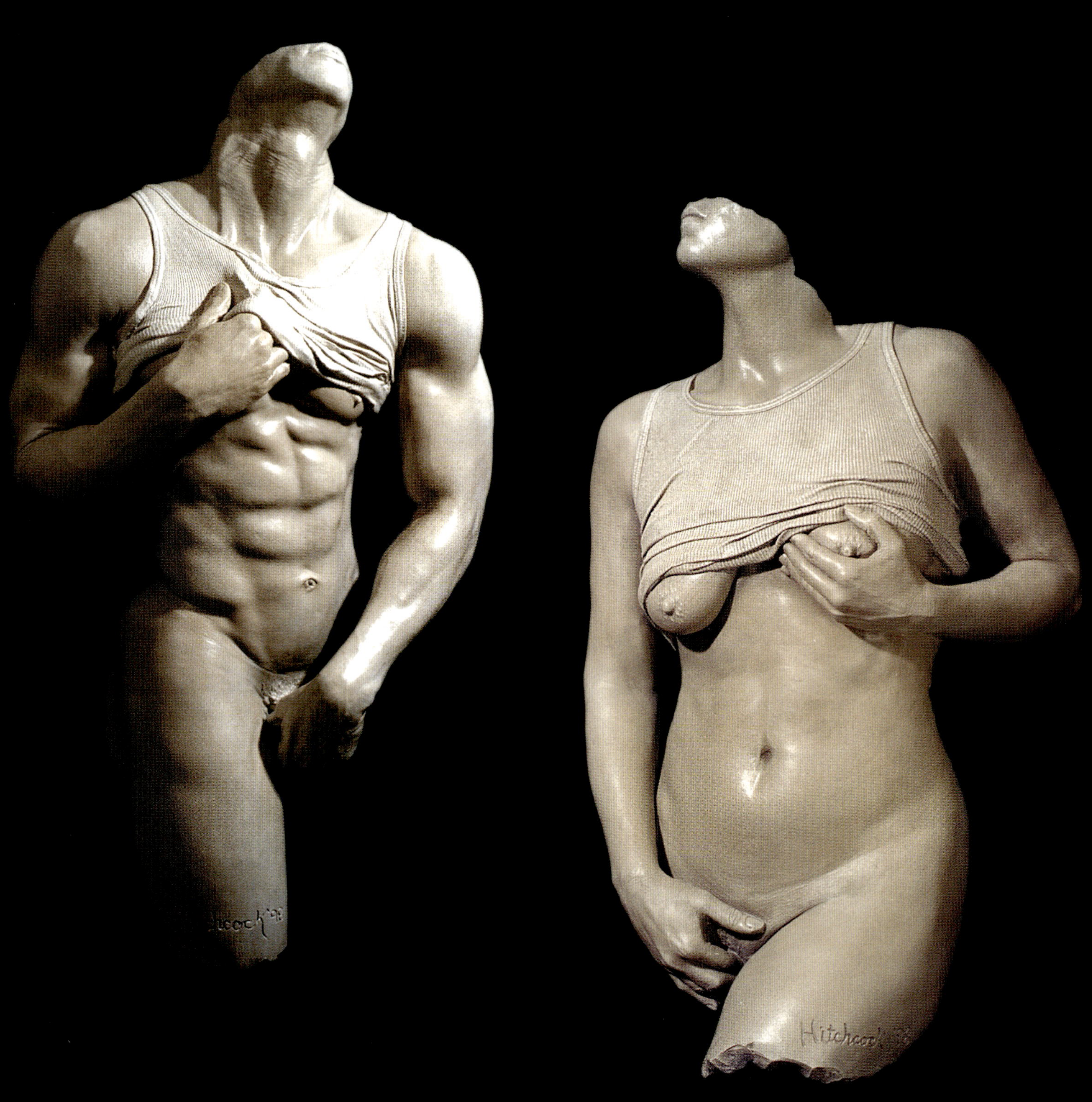
Hitchcock '98

FLIGHT, 1999
cast gypsum,
26" x 26" x 12"

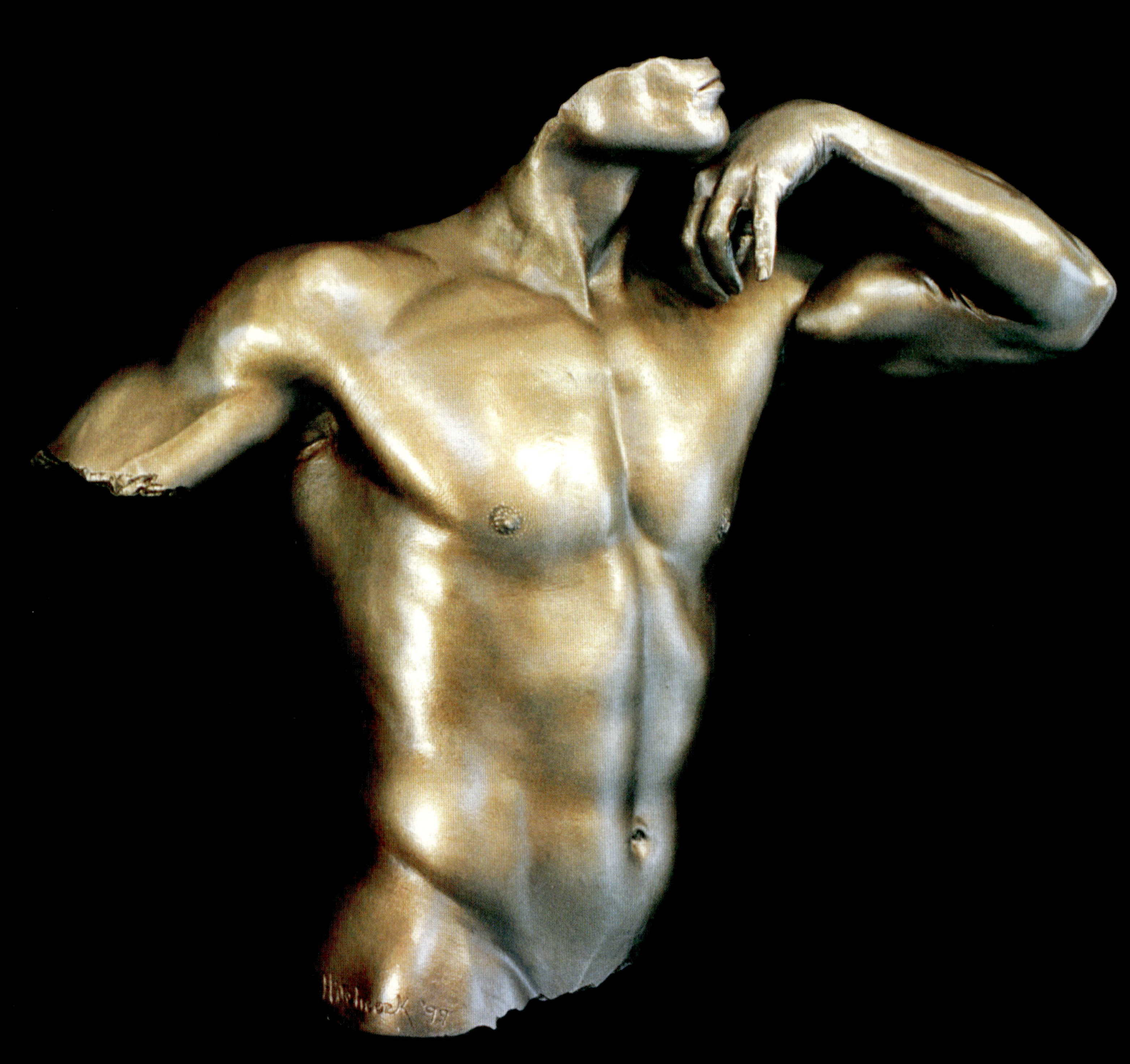

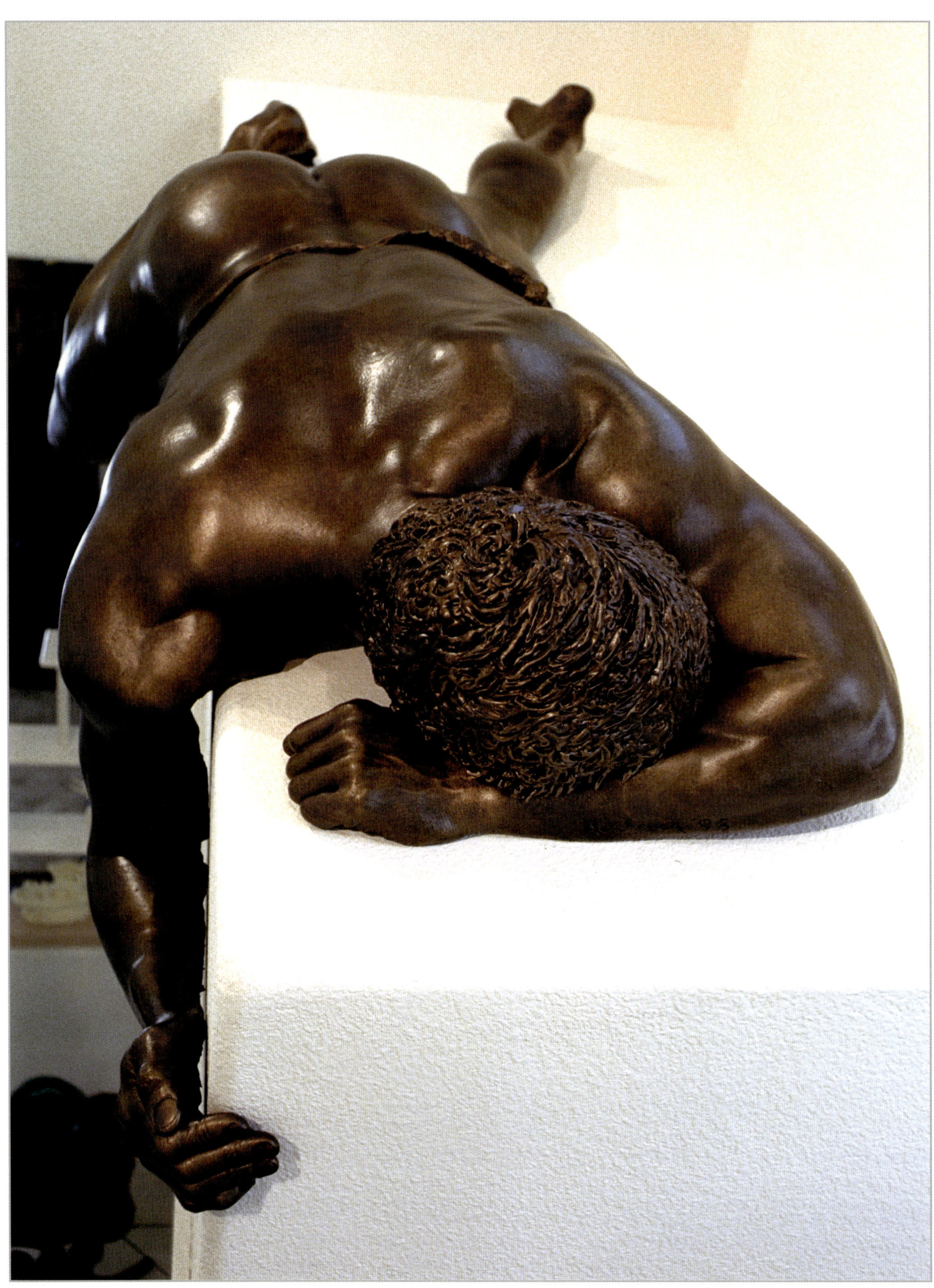

FALLEN IDOL, 1998
cast gypsum, fiberglass,
30" x 72" x 32"
(detail above)

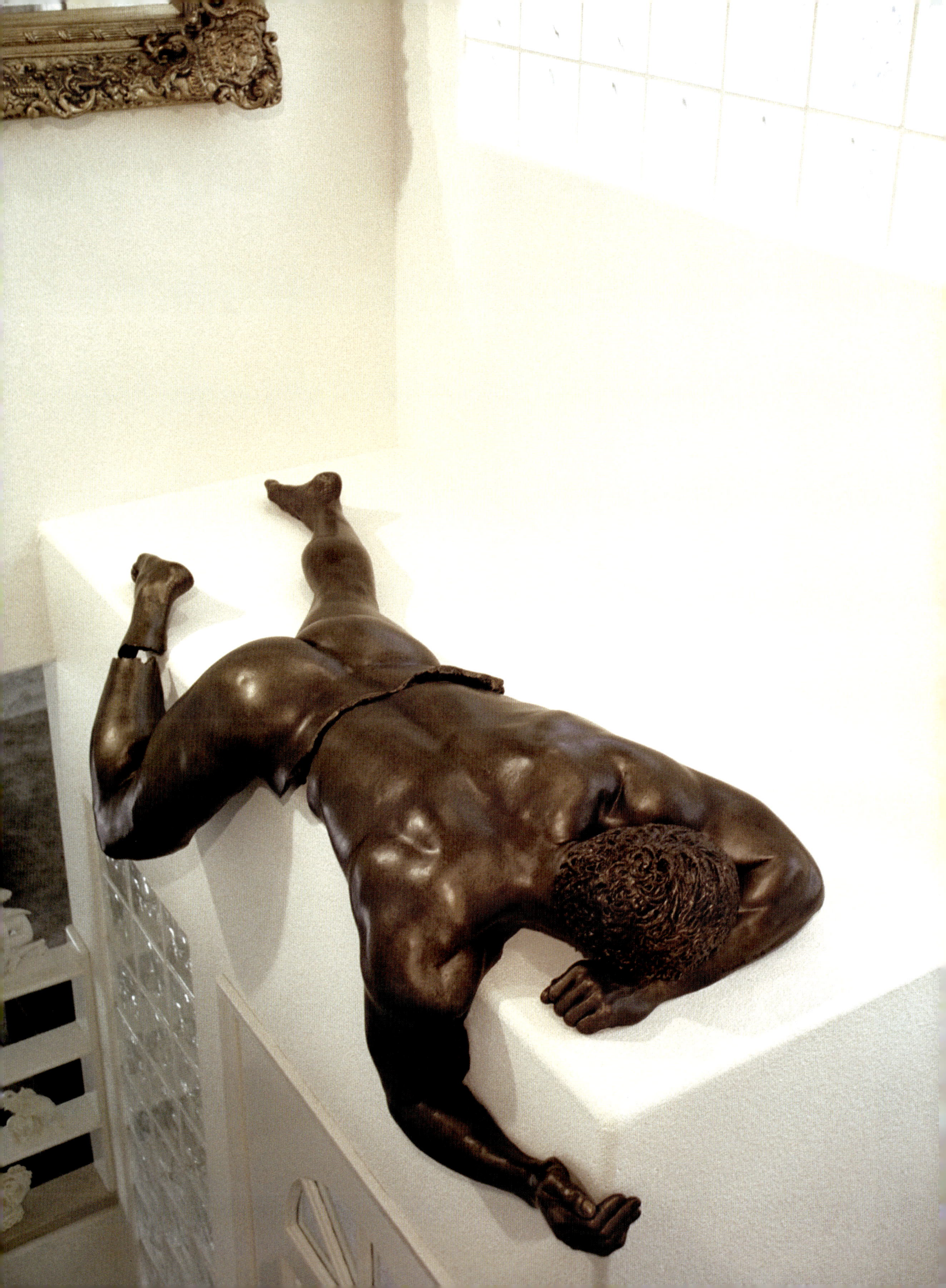

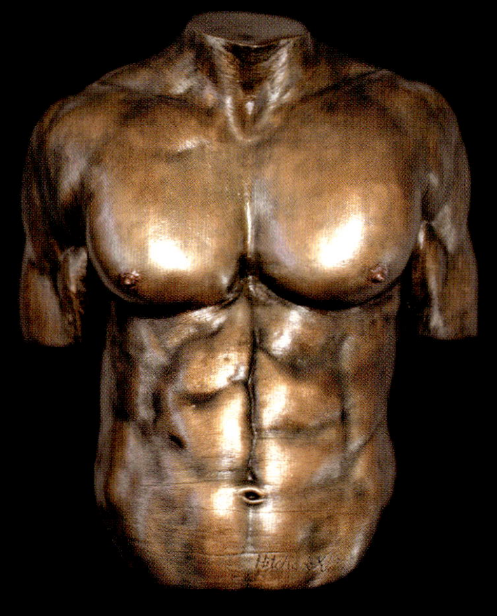

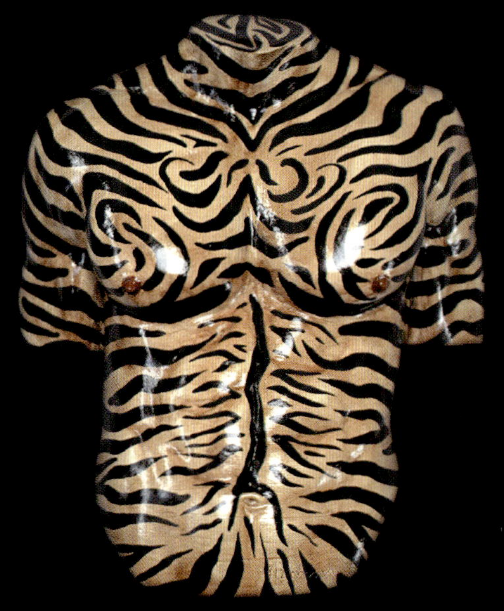

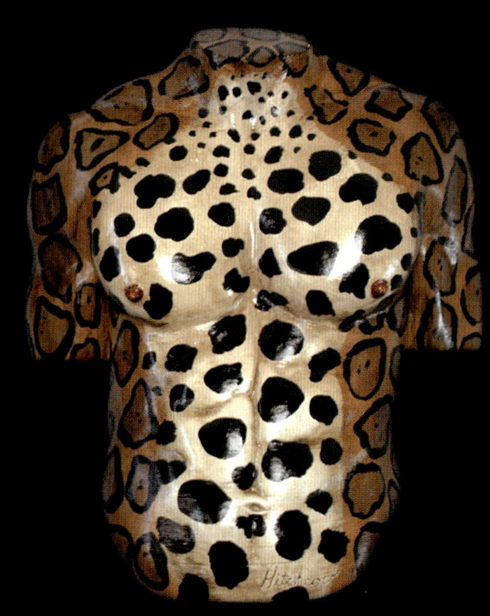

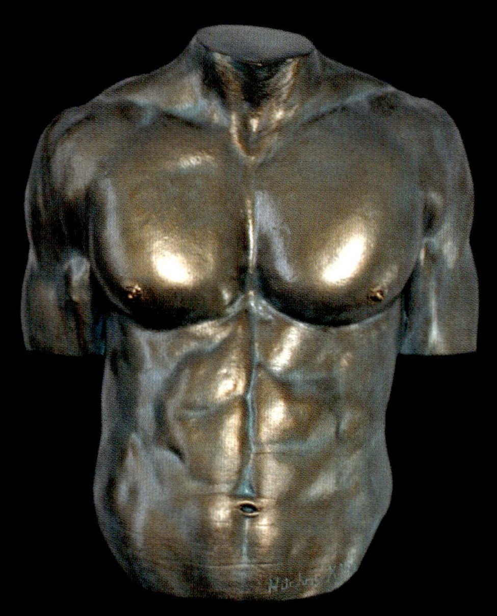

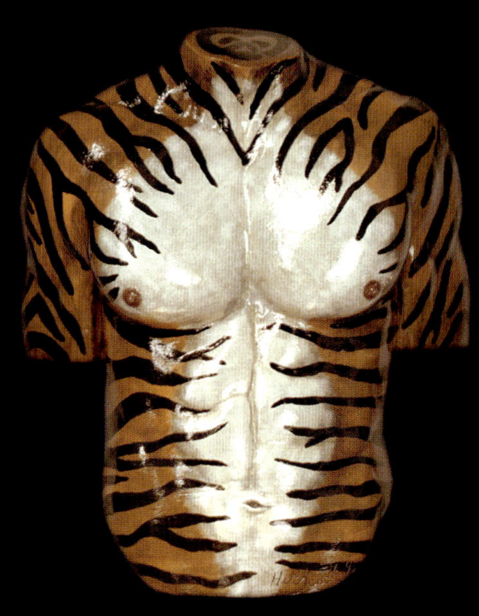

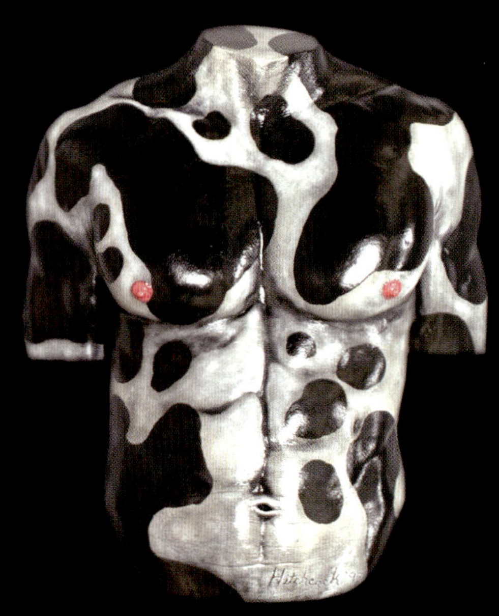

ANIMALS & ANTIQUES, 1994
THE MALE TORSO AS CANVAS
acrylic on cast gypsum,
32" x 24" x 12" each

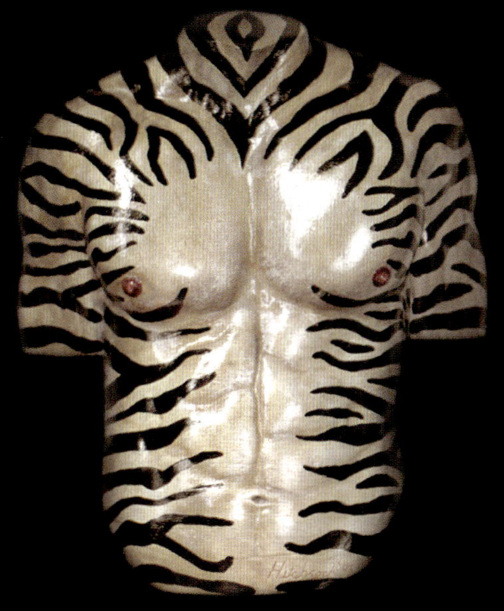

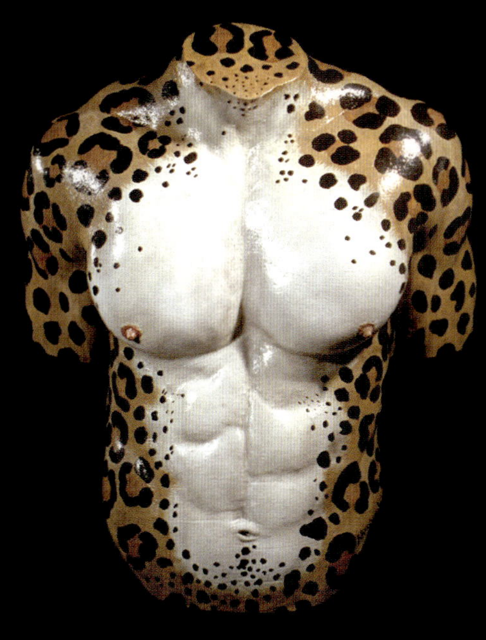

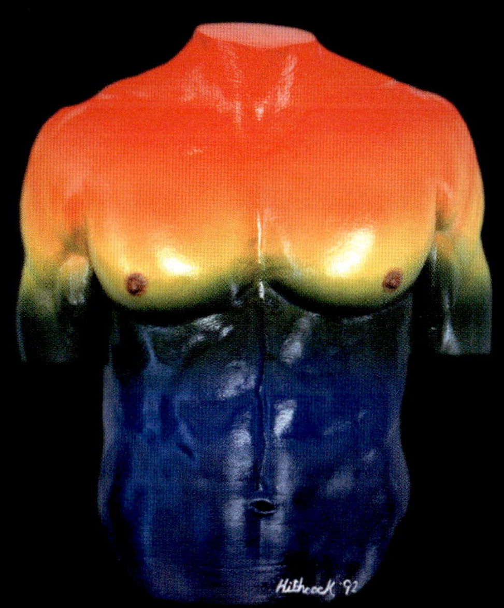
Hithcock '92

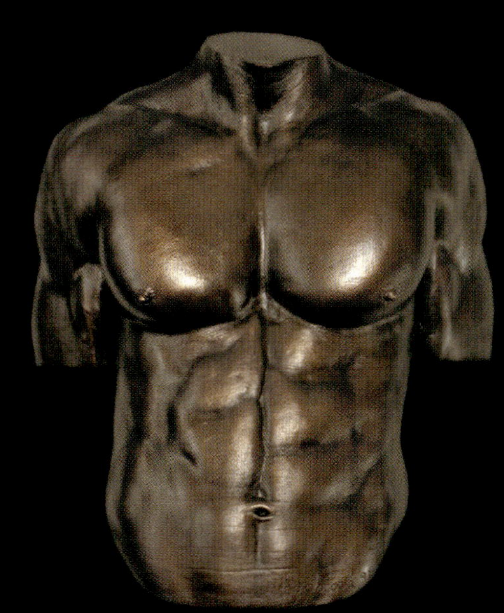

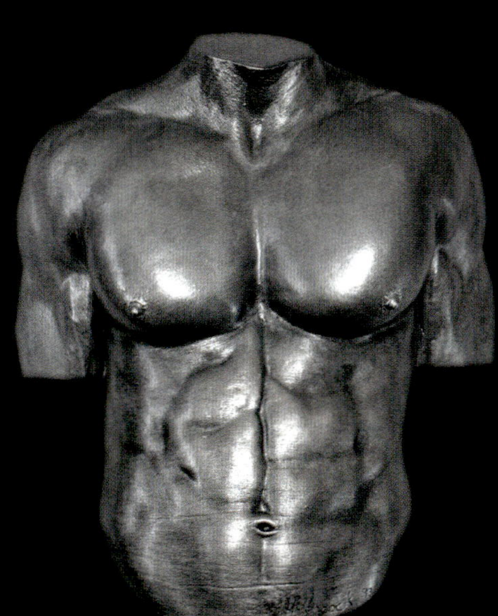

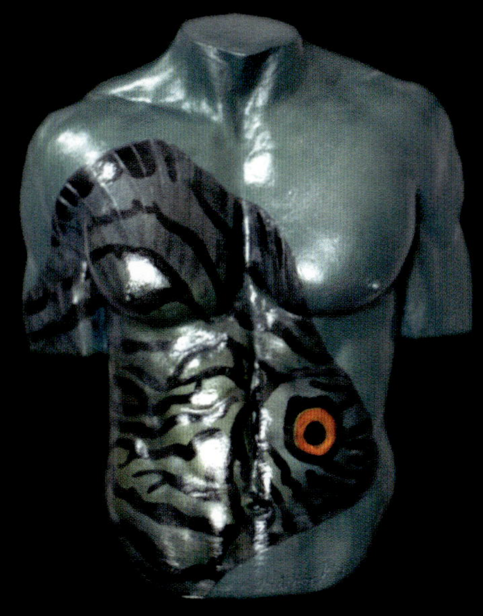

JAMIE, 1996
cast gypsum,
36” x 24” x 14”

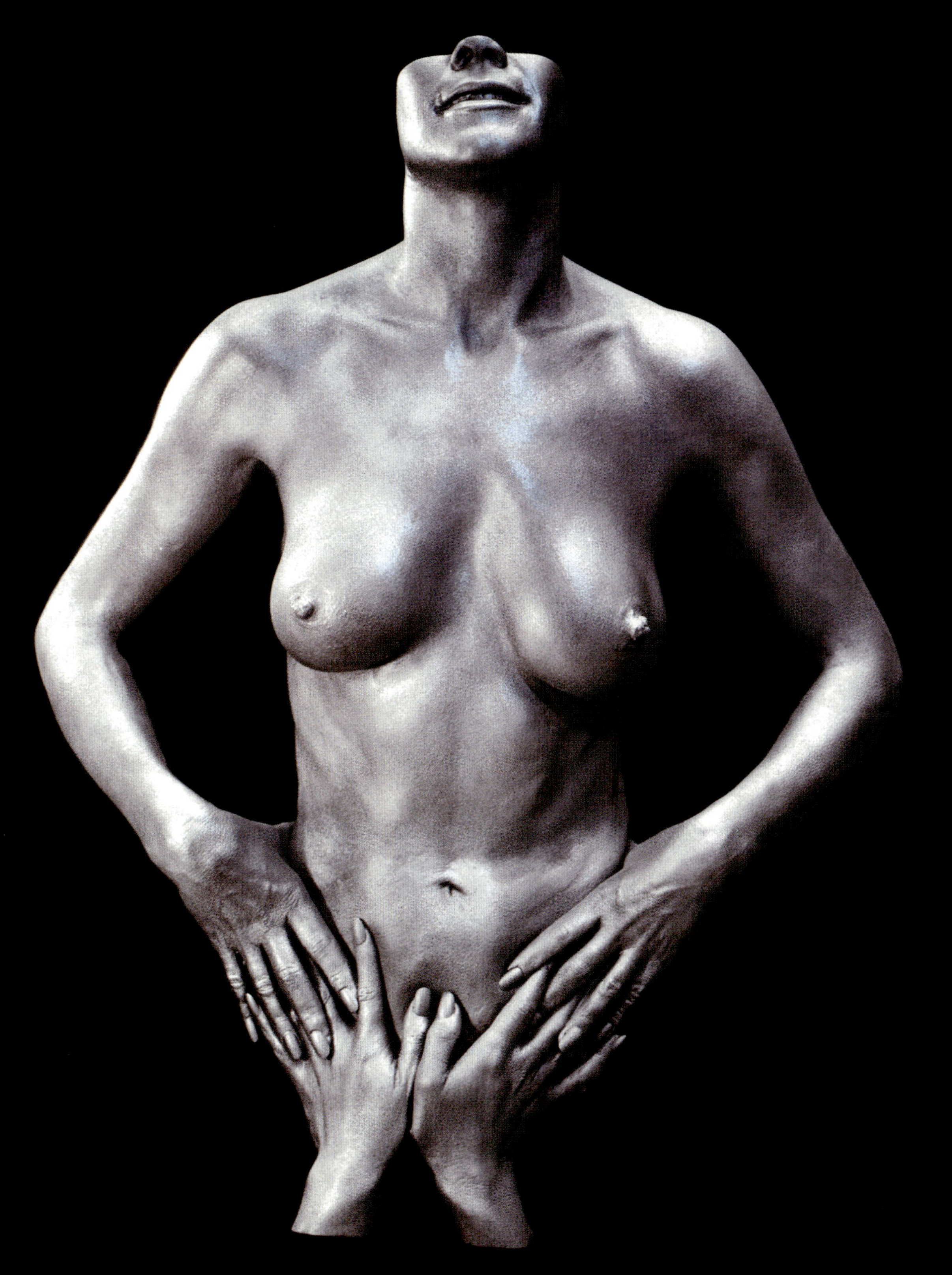

LYNN, 1997
cast gypsum,
36” x 24” x 20”

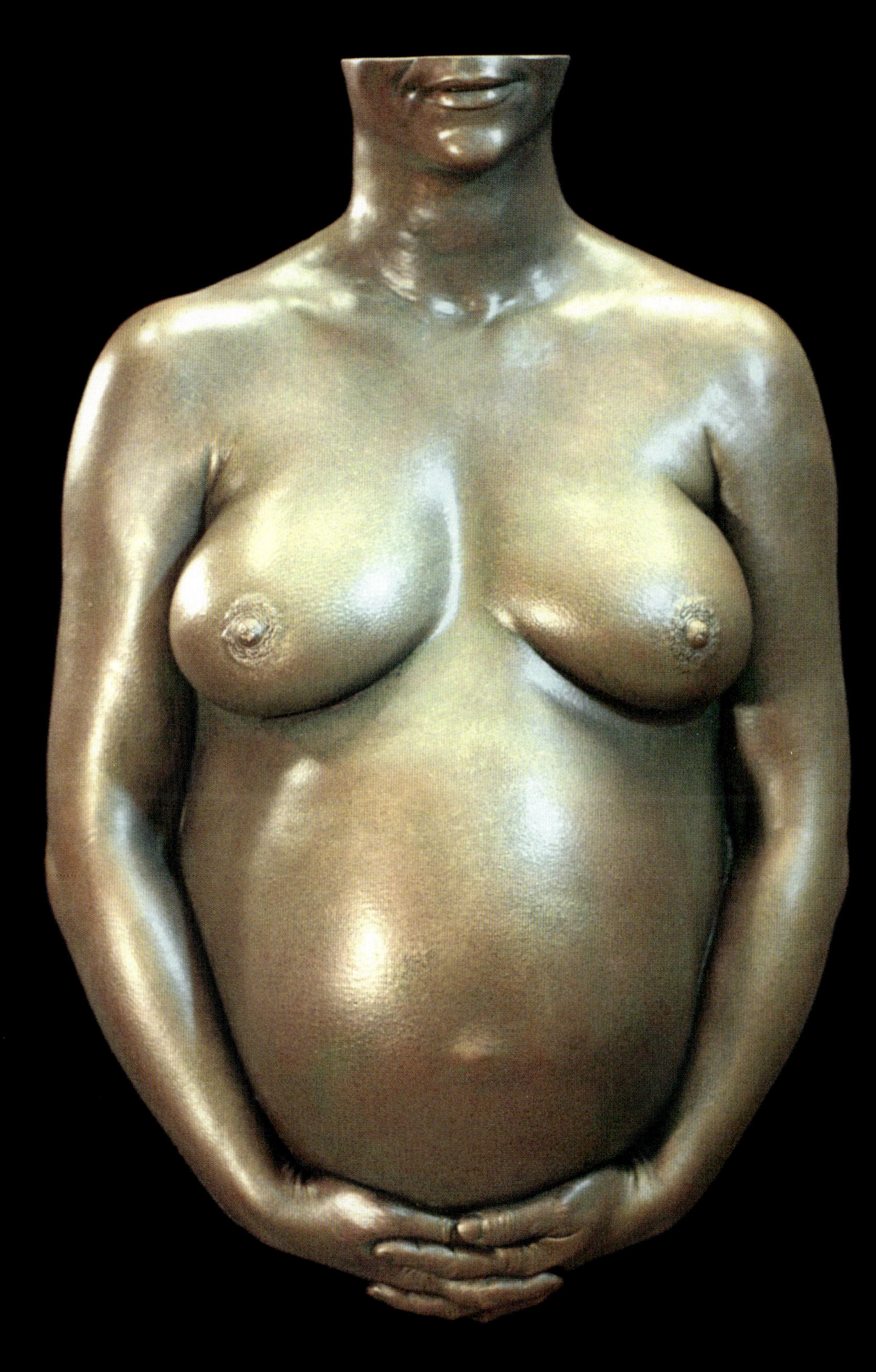

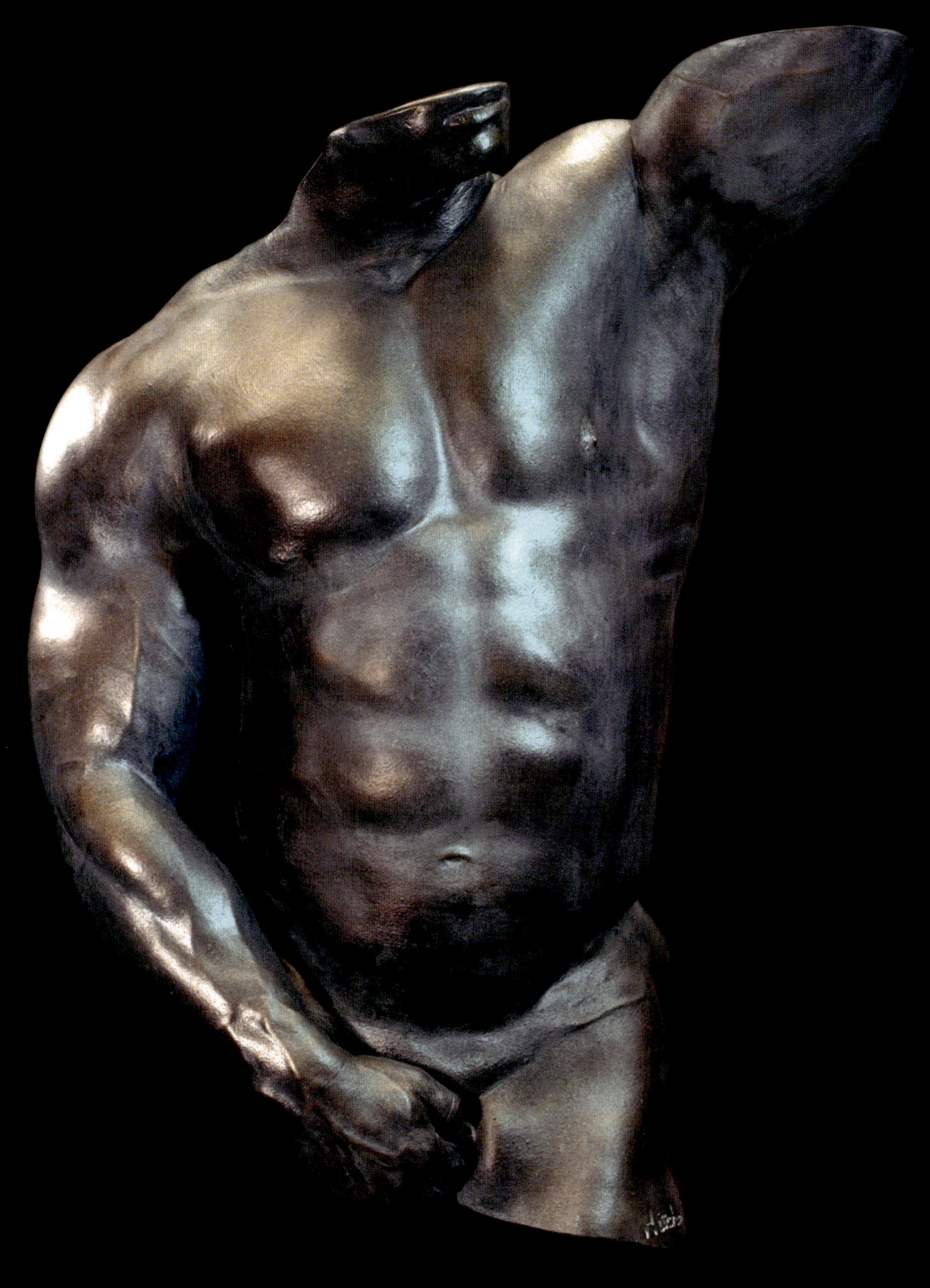

BRIAN & JOEY, 1996
cast gypsum,
36” x 26” x 14” each

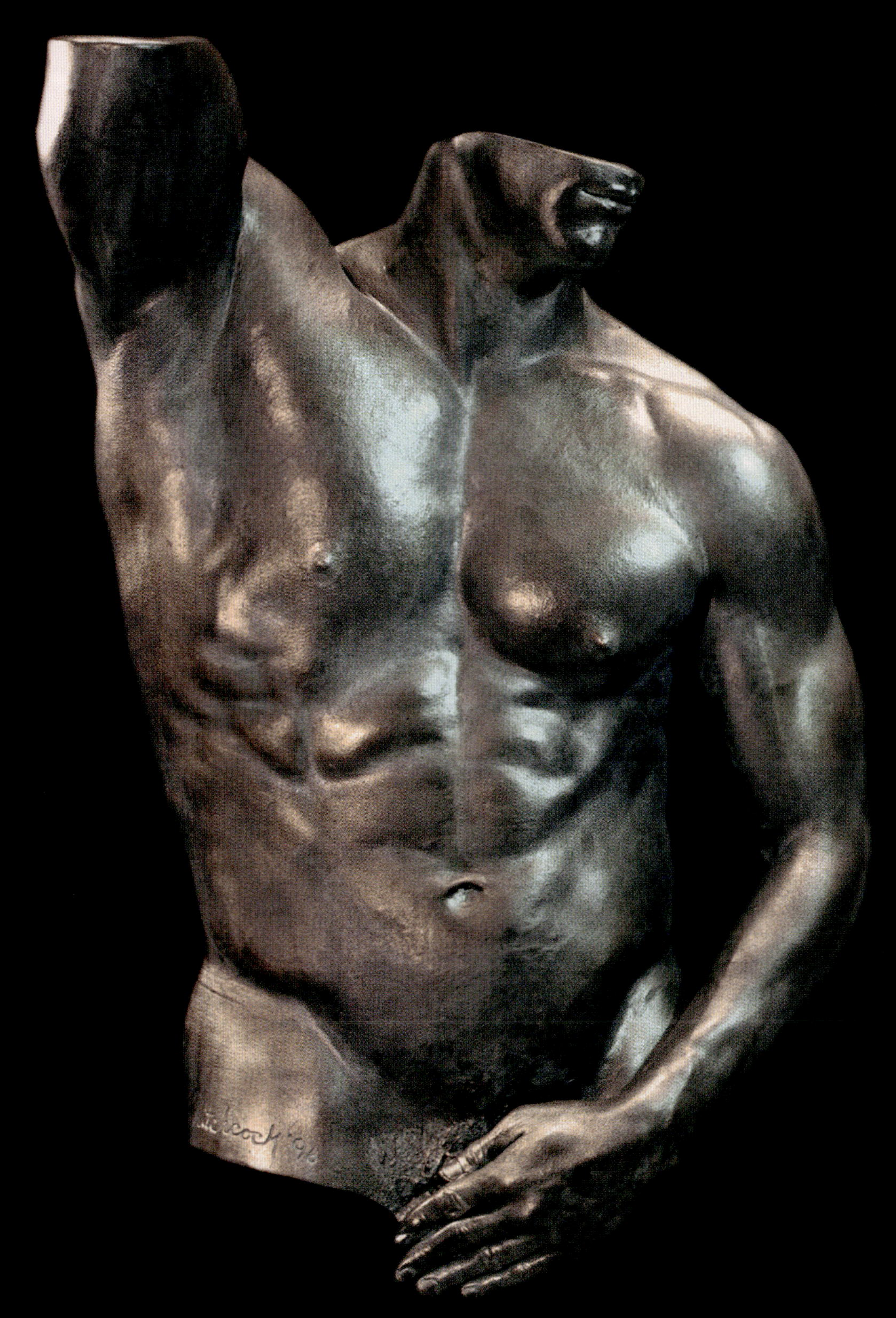

CENTAUR & LAPITH YOUTH, 1995
cast gypsum
24" x 18" x 12"

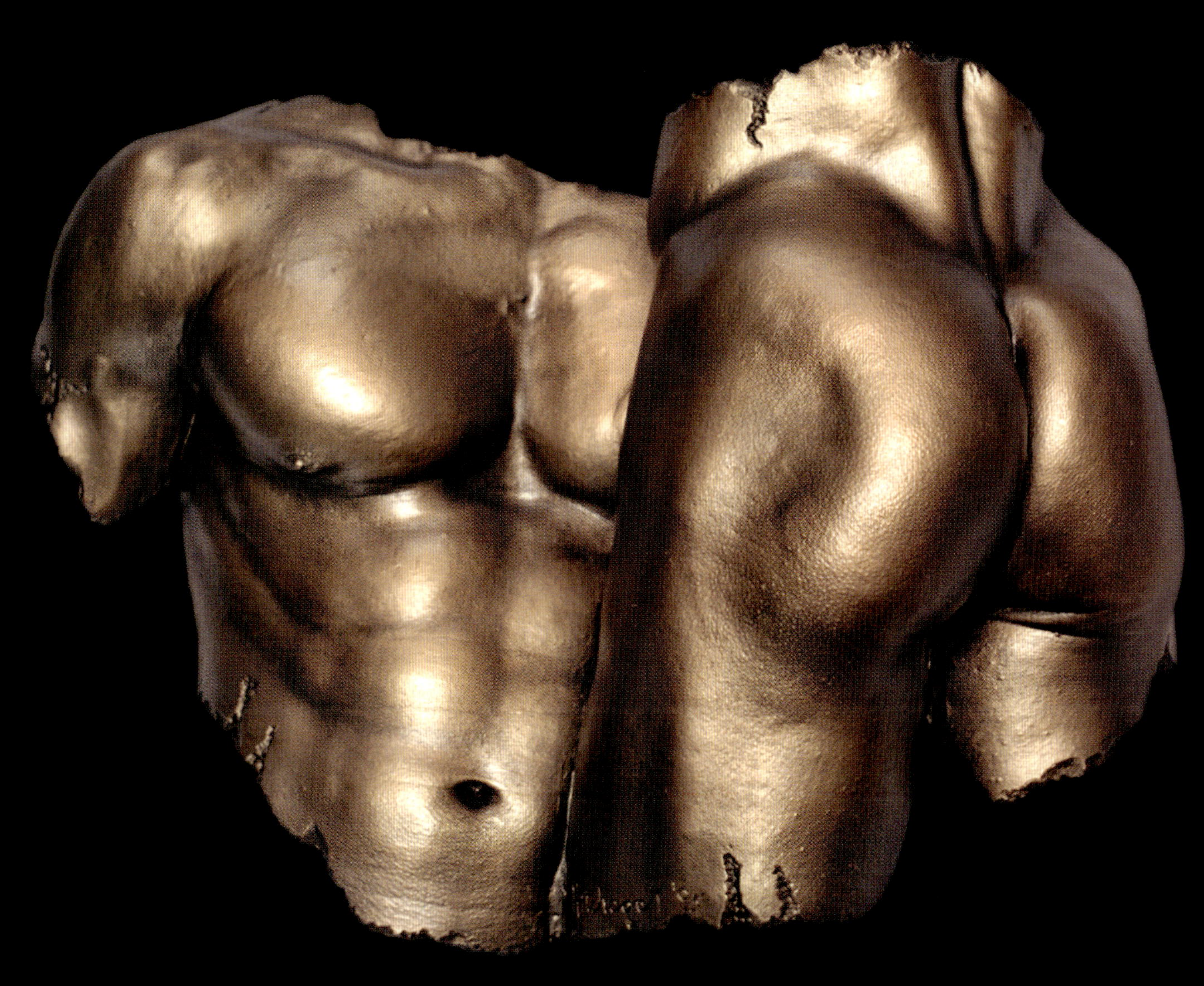

VENUS, 1999
cast gypsum, steel, mink skull,
30” x 18” x 12”

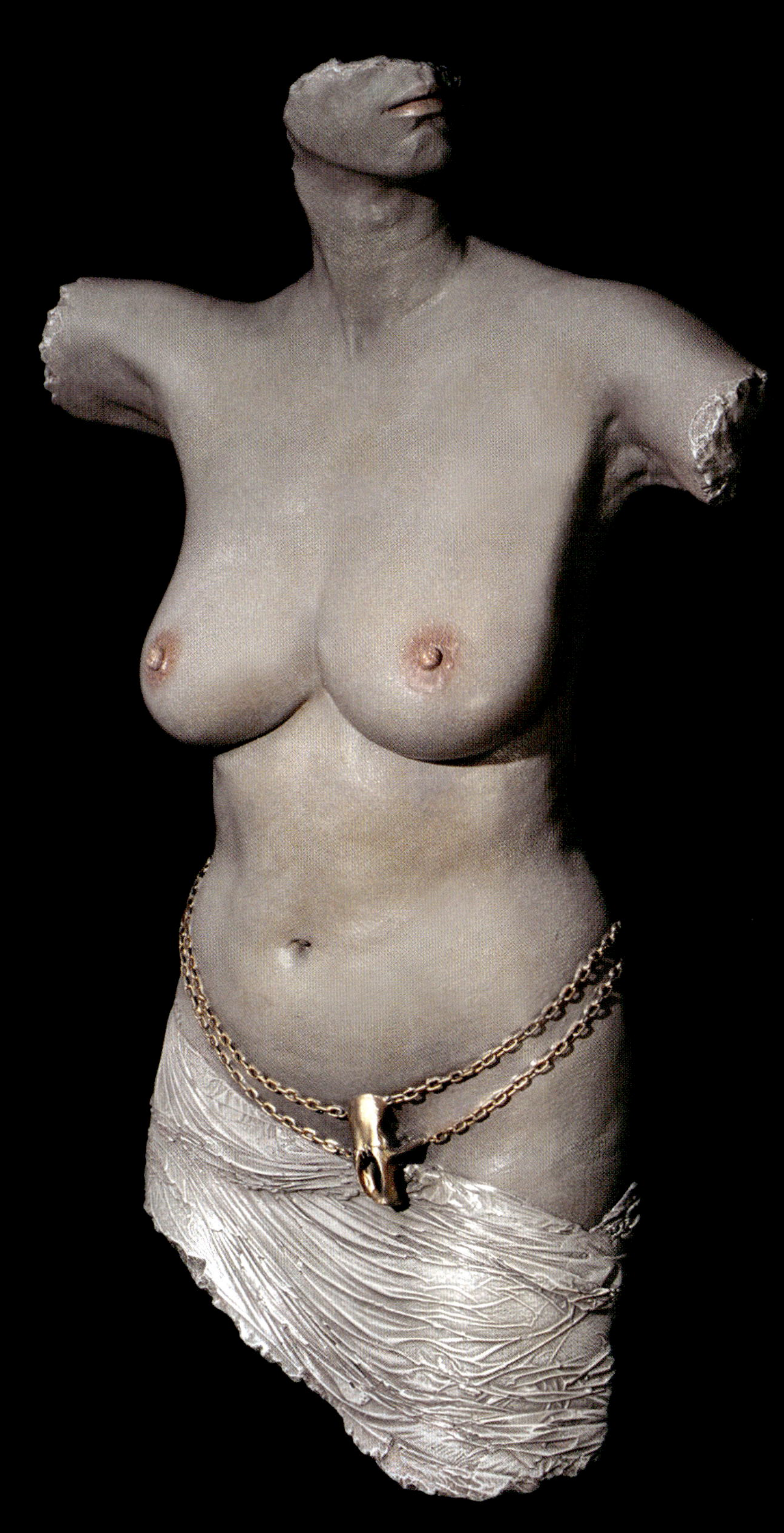

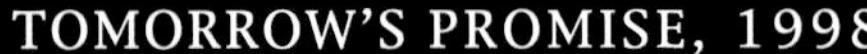

TOMORROW'S PROMISE, 1998
cast gypsum, wood,
60" x 30" x 14" *Model: Joseph Myska*

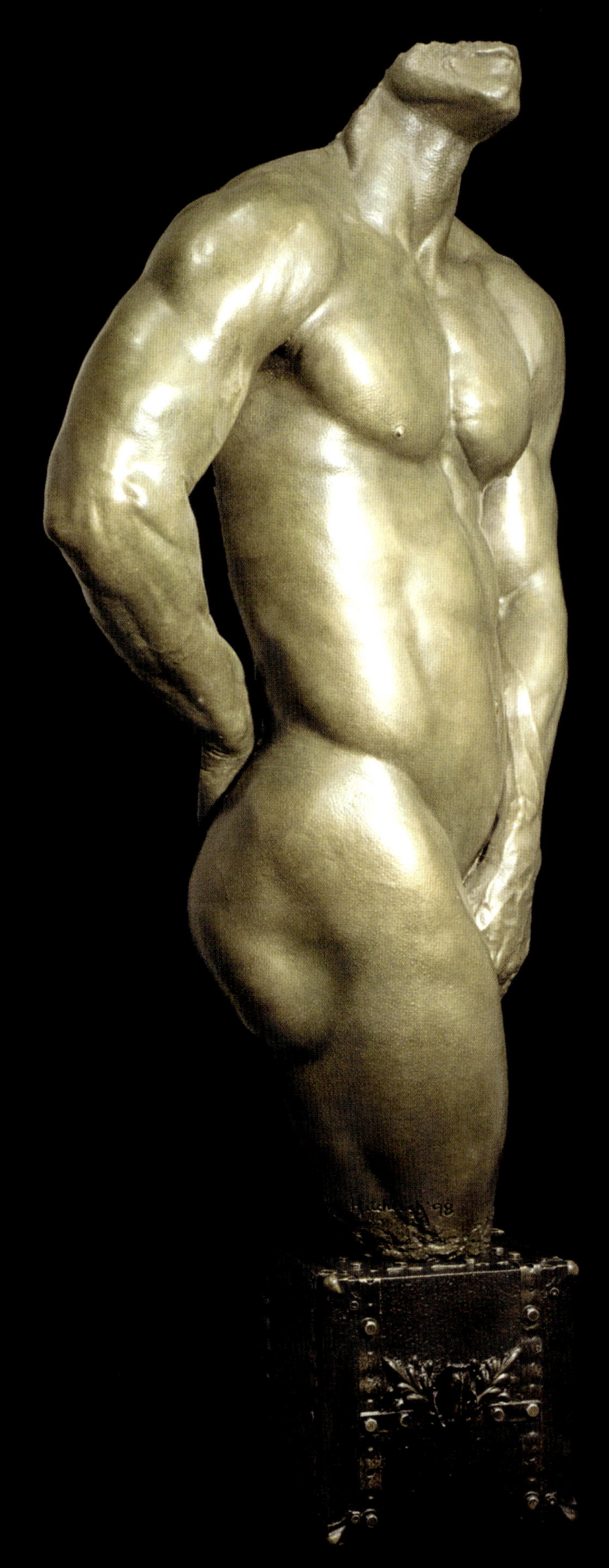

TORSO OBELISK, 1999
cast gypsum,
60" x 18" x 18"

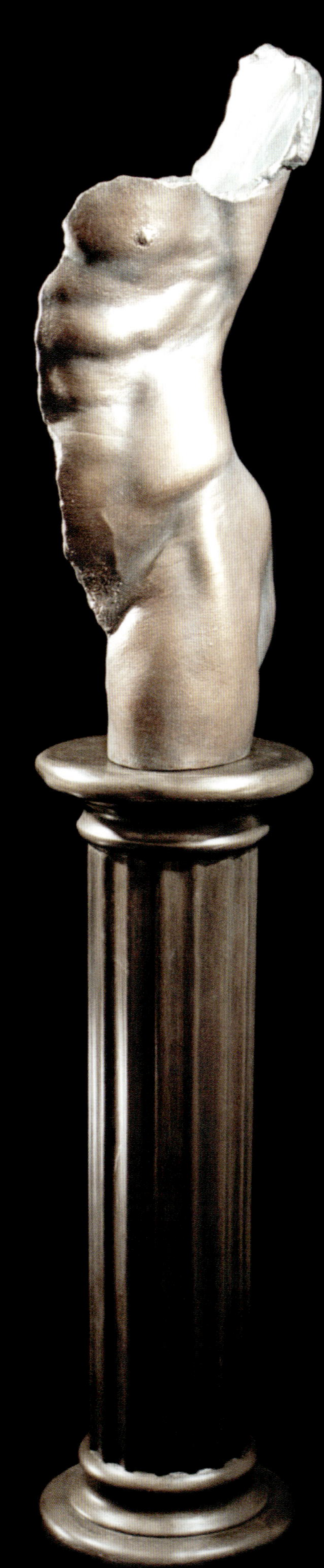

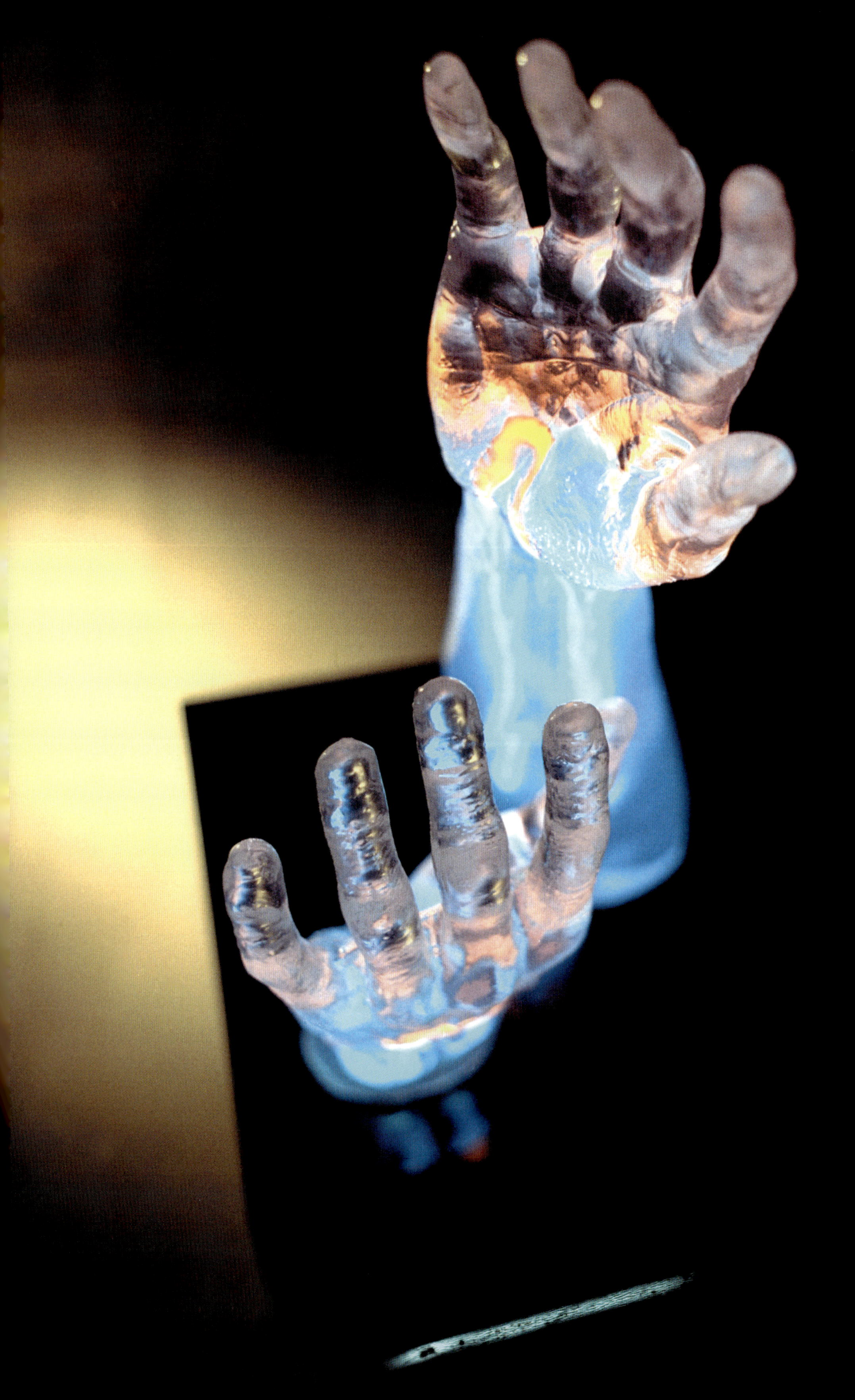

UNTITLED HANDS, 1991
cast resin, neon tubes,
18” x 9” x 9”

FAMILY CIRCLE, 1994
cast resin, steel, neon,
42" x42" x 14" *Model: Barbie Benton & Family*

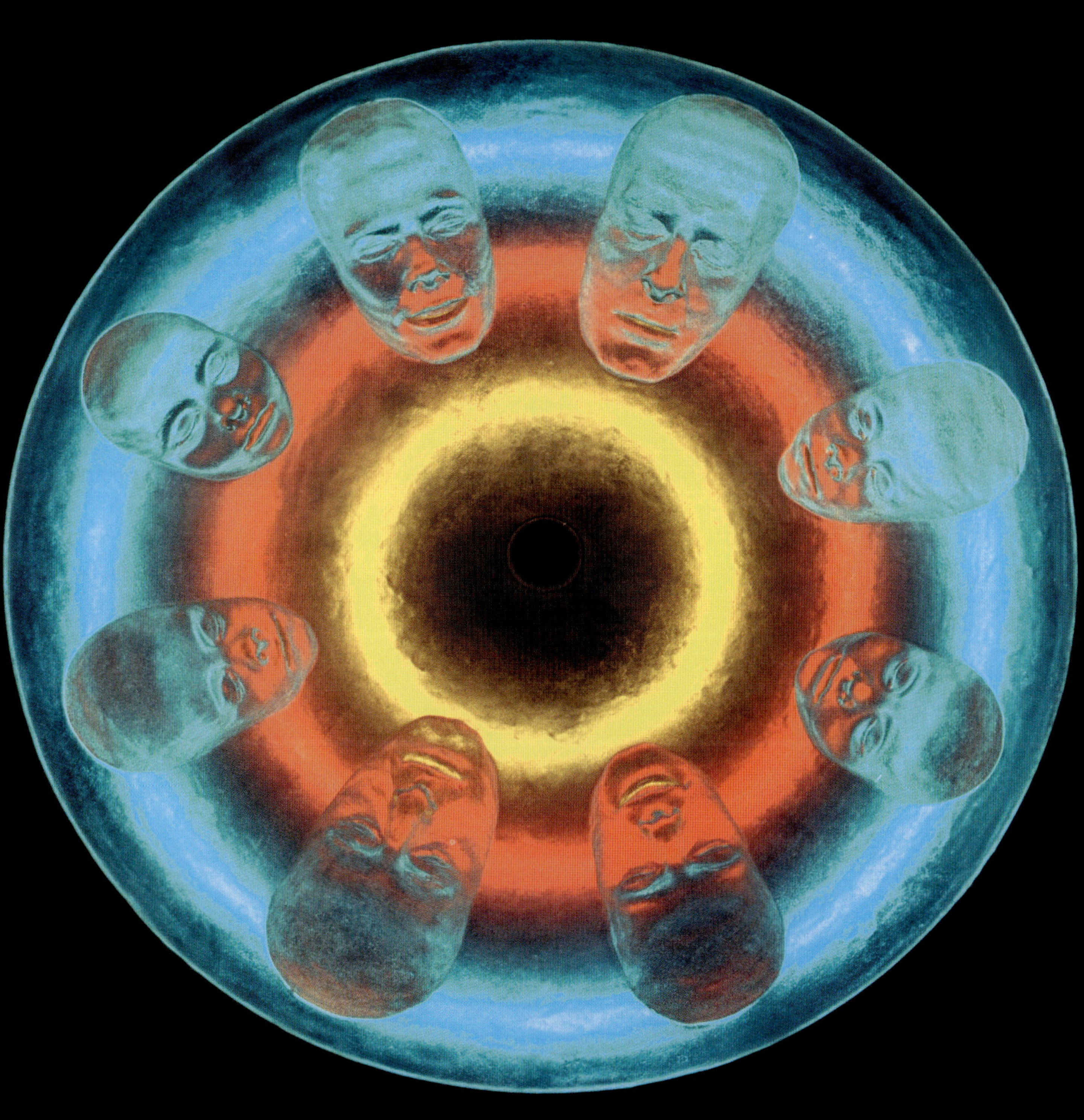

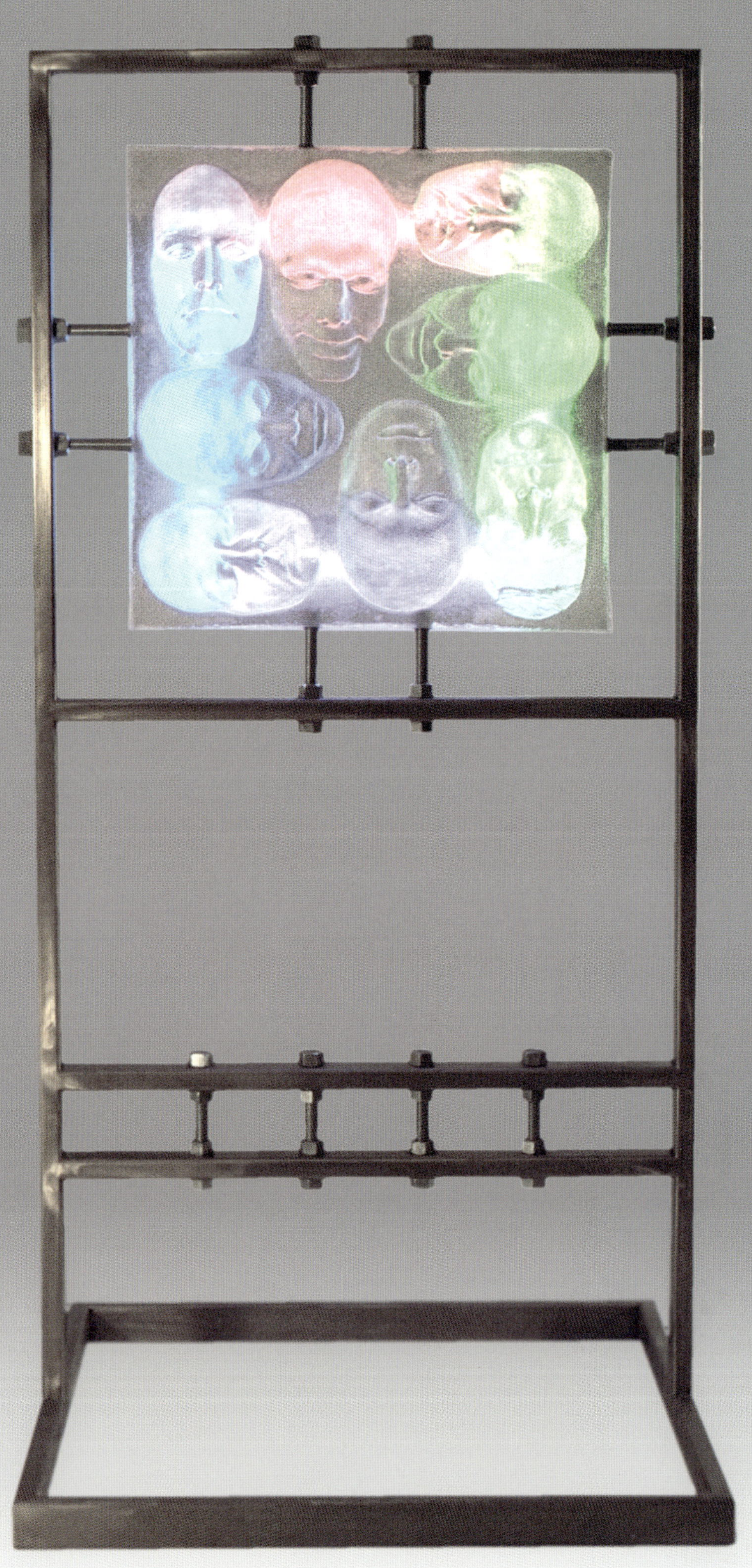

BIOPSY, 1993
cast resin, steel, neon,
60" x 30" x 30"

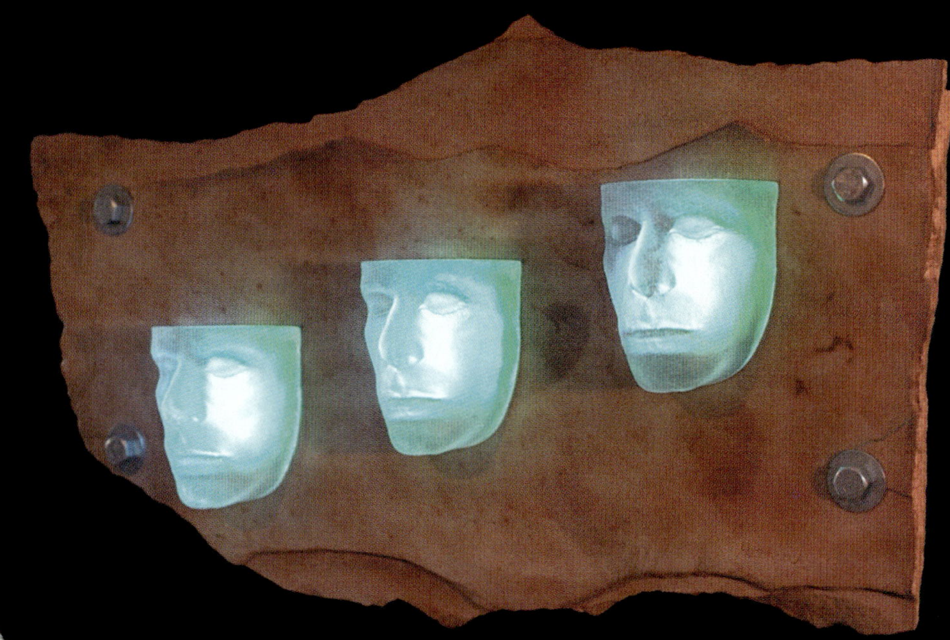

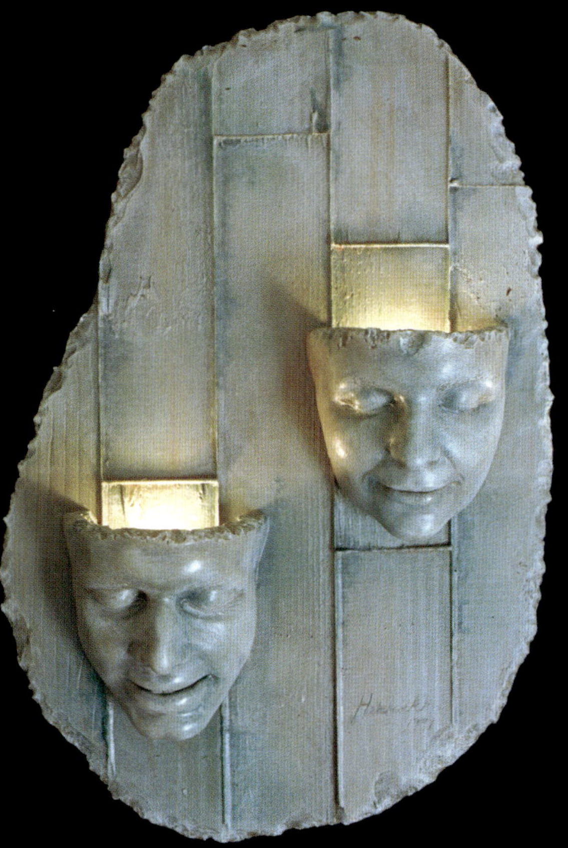

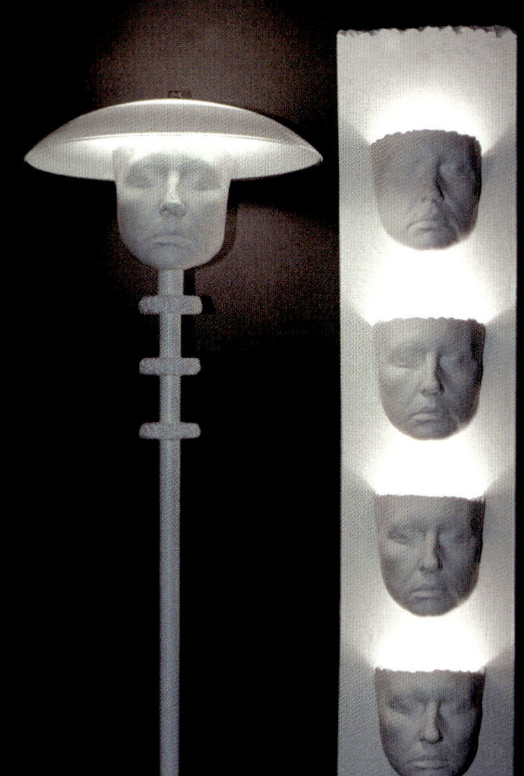

(clockwise from left)
HAPPY URBAN COUPLE, 1991
cast gypsum, incandescent lights,
28" x 18" x 6"

RONNIE, 1993
cast resin, neon, flagstone,
14" x 34" x 8"

DEE DEE, 1990
cast gypsum, steel, incandescent lights,
60" x 10" x 8"

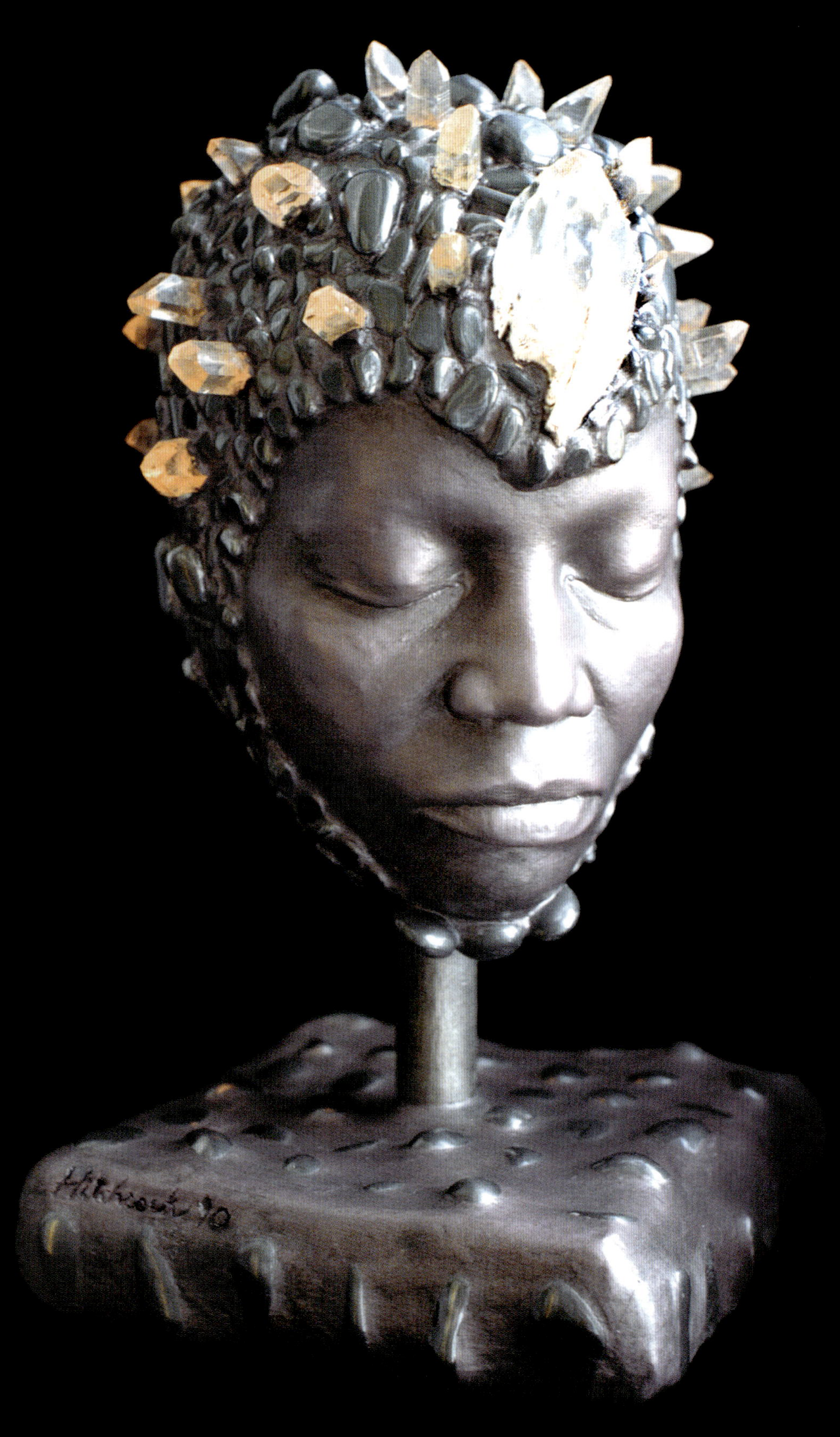

THE RECEIVER, 1990
cast gypsum, quartz, hematite, incandescent light,
14" x 9" x 9"

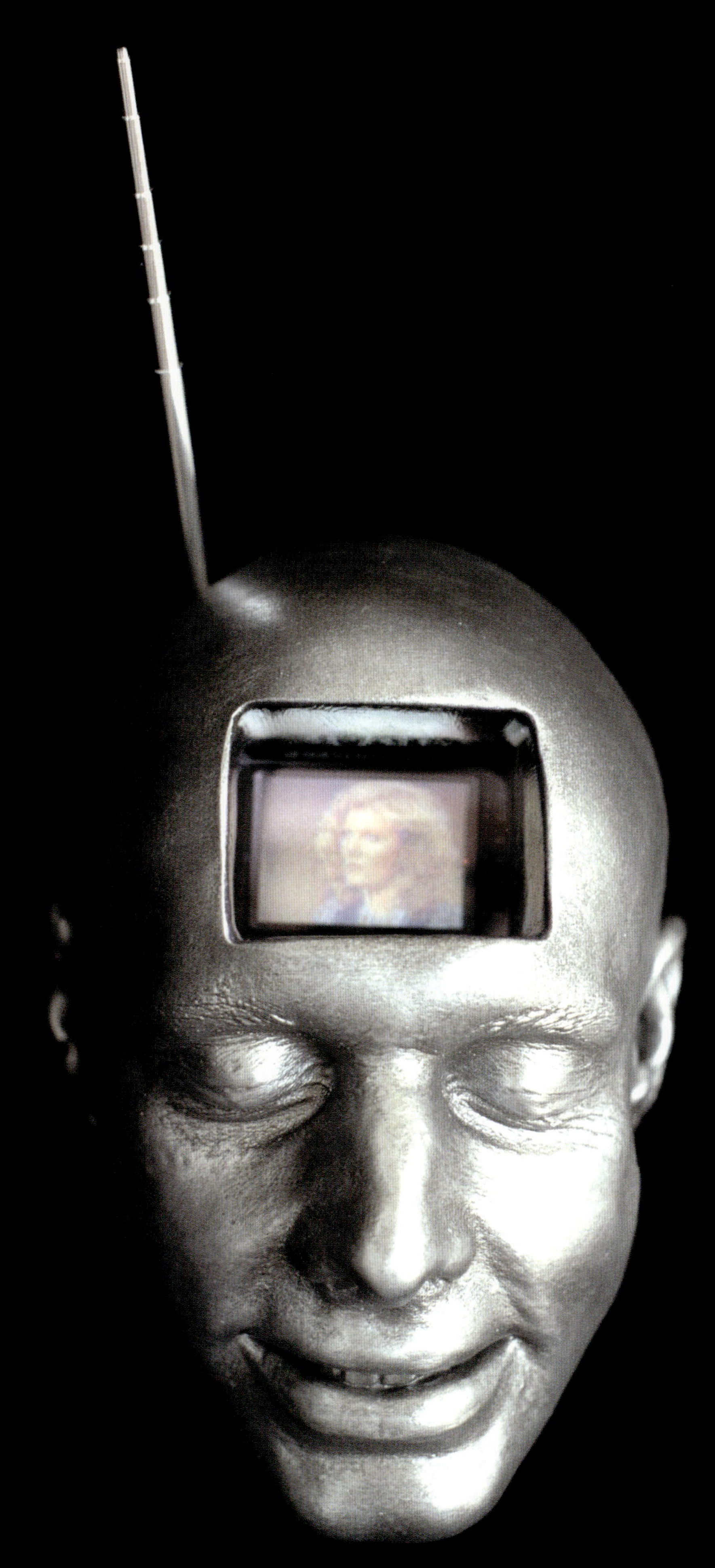

BRAIN TUMOR, 1991
cast gypsum, miniature color TV,
10" x 8" x 8"

ILLUMINATION, 1989
cast gypsum, wood,
18" x 72" x 14"

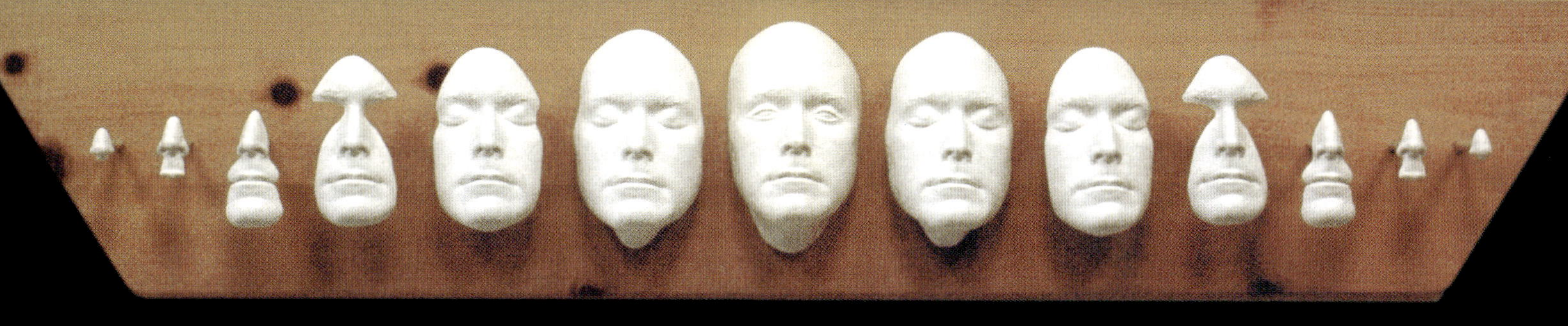

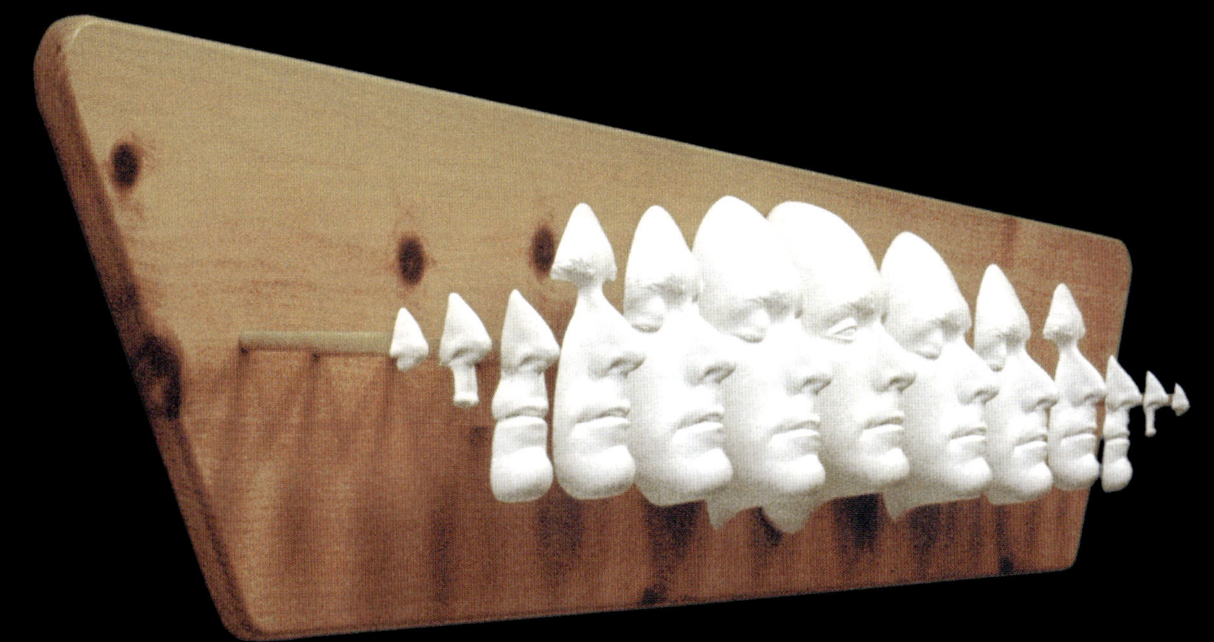

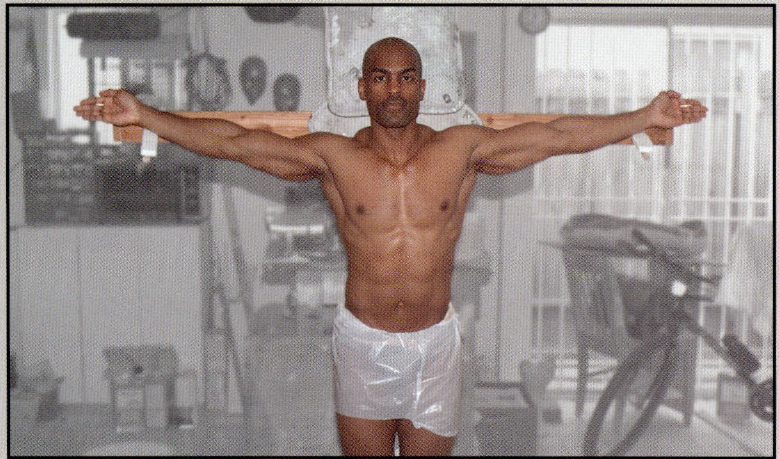

Photo 1-The selection of a pose is critical to a successful cast. The body is positioned as you would have gravity effect it. Therefore a vertically situated sculpture does not begin with a reclining model, but rather with one which stands. Due to the difficulty of the pose, a scaffold has been built to support the model's arms during the 25 minute process.

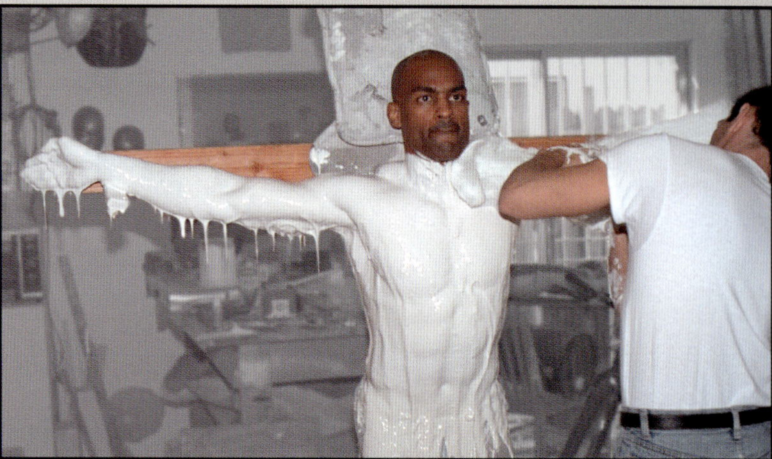

Photo 2- Alginate is applied to the subject. The 4 minute gel time is extended by activating the alginate with cold water. The expression on the face of the model is an indication of temperature!

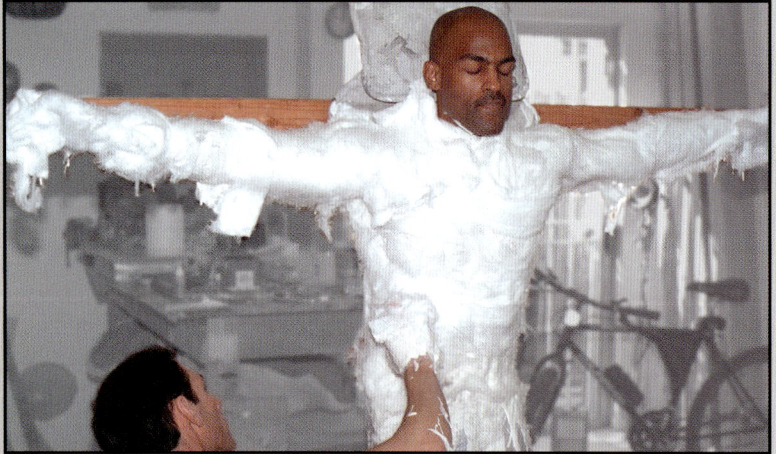

Photo 3- Cotton is pushed into the alginate before it gels. The excess cotton is removed, leaving a fibrous surface that will enable the mother mold to adhere.

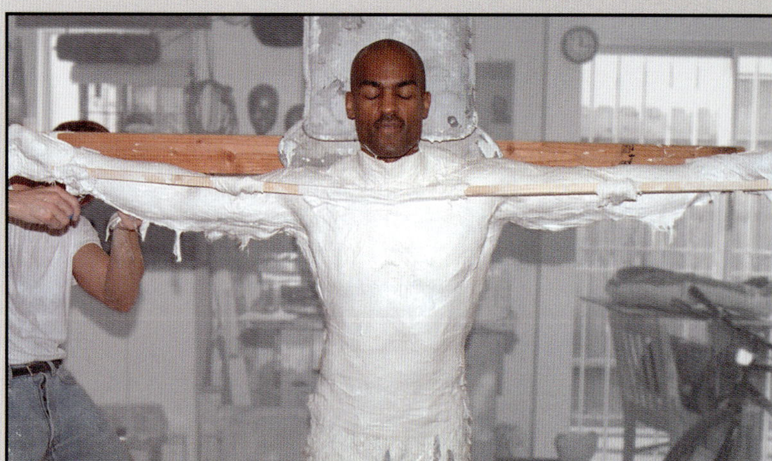

Photo 4- Plaster gauze is used to give rigidity to an otherwise flimsy mold. Wooden splints add further reinforcement. (Is my model losing steam?!)

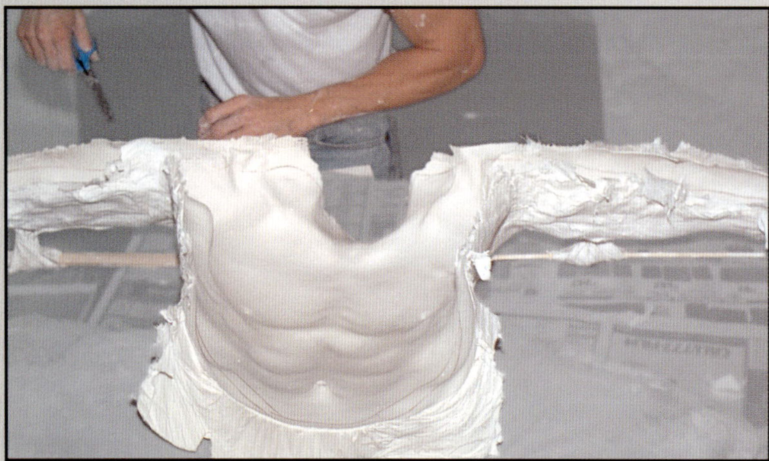

Photo 5- The finished negative mold is removed and trimmed for casting. Since the mold is literally torn away from the finished cast, it can be used only once.

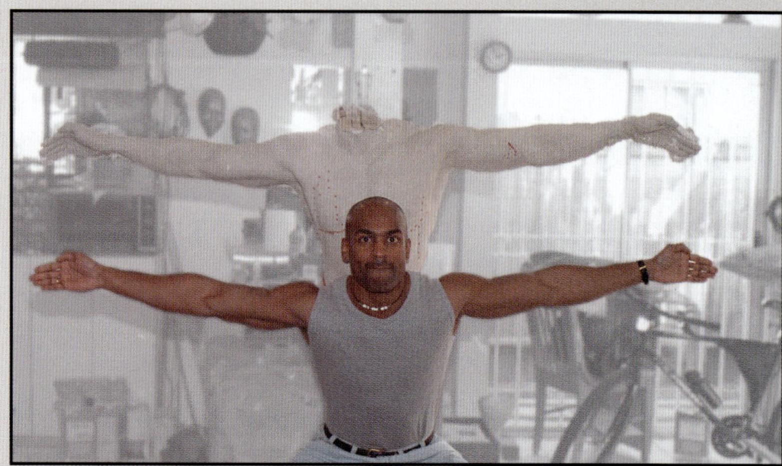

Photo 6- The "raw pull" is removed from the mold. Lifecasting is frequently an imperfect process. Small dots show areas that need to be re-sculpted.

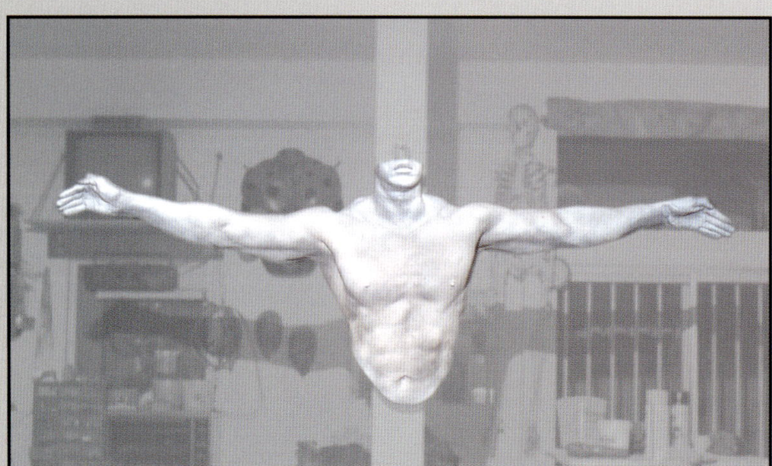

Photo 7- The cast torso has been completely corrected and refined. Note that a portion of a face has been added to give the piece more character and life. The cast is sealed with a primer.

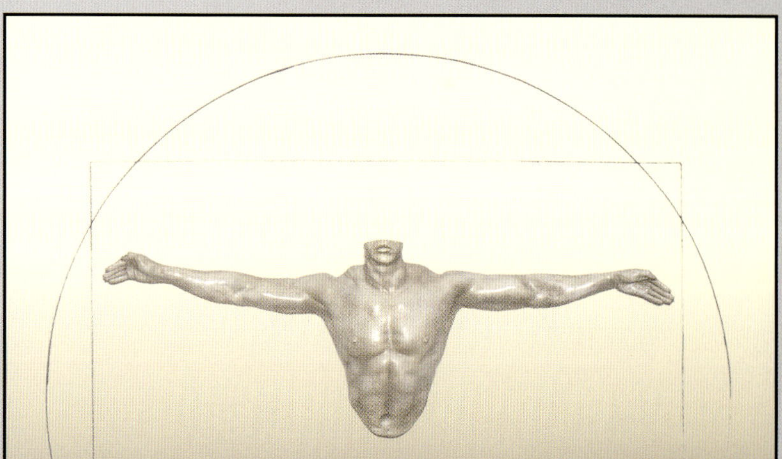

Photo 8: The Finished Piece- An antique Limestone patina has been applied to the piece aptly titled, "The Cannon of Proportion," inspired by the famous drawings of Leonardo Da Vinci. During this exhibit, The "square in the circle" was scribed onto the wall.

About the Process of Casting from Life...

by Philip Hitchcock

In 1877, Auguste Rodin exhibited his sculpture "The Age of Bronze" at the Paris Salon. The statue created an instant scandal among critics because they refused to believe that Rodin could create such a realistic sculpture without using a cast of a live model. So incensed was one naysayer that he hung a sign on the statue which read "Molded from the model!"

Lifecasting, the process of replicating shapes from human models, has a rich and somewhat controversial history in the art world. Though many still regard it as craft or technique, a number of artists (myself included) have elevated the process to real artistic expression. In fact, the best "lifecasting" incorporates many elements of traditional sculpture. So to spare Monsieur Rodin any further controversy, let us define sculpture simply as the creation of any three-dimensional form, in the round or in relief, and let us count lifecasting among the many techniques available to that process.

The oldest known lifecast is over three thousand years old and dates back to Roman days. Upon death, a statesman's "Deathmask" was made as a three-dimensional reference for carving a marble bust. (One marketing note here: A LIFEcast is a much easier sell than a DEATHmask!) Before the french art critics would *accuse* Rodin of lifecasting, Madame Toussaud had already become notorious for casting the guillotined heads of famous criminals to create figures for her wax museum. In America, The sculptor Volk made casts of Abraham Lincoln's face and hands to create a portrait of the young statesman. He had Lincoln hold a broom handle in his right hand and make a fist with his left. These casts took on such great significance, that they were copied over the years in many different forms and eventually became the guide for the Lincoln Memorial in Washington D.C. In more recent times, lifecasting has been used as a basis for creating prosthetics for medical and dental applications. Hollywood has also made great use of lifecasting to create special effects for movies. But several artists have used this technique as an art form unto itself. George Segal used plaster gauze to make "shell molds" from models and then assembled them into full figures. In this technique, the gauze applied to the body became the actual positive. Still others used materials to create negative molds from their subjects that were later cast in positive form to create life-like figures. The best known of these artists was Duane Hansen, who created amazingly realistic figures in vinyl, some which are virtually indistinguishable from their human counterparts! Willa Shallit has also been a ground breaker. She founded the "Touch Museum" where blind people are encouraged to touch the lifemasks of famous people so they might "see" how they look. Her work is distinguished by the emphasis she places on the frozen moment in time and the communion between artist and model.

Though many people are fascinated by the intensely personal aspects of casting an individual's face, I try to objectify the body, to make it more like architecture. The sculpture becomes more *personality neutral* and more universally accessible. The work is less about the model's identity and more about my message as an artist.

"So what do you do?... just kinda' lay somebody down in plaster?"

I hear this question all the time and the person asking it is usually very serious. The thinking behind this question is wrong on so many levels that it's difficult to know where to begin. Let me say, first of all, that with the state of the art being what it is, no one should be using plaster to make a mold from a human model! It requires a vat of Vaseline and a near motionless subject. Additionally, plaster is so brittle and without flex, that large human casts are nearly impossible. The heat generated by plaster, or worse hydrocal, causes unnecessary discomfort to the model and in some cases burns! So, if someone ever offers to "plaster" you in this fashion, my advice to you is ....RUN! The only exception to this would be the use of plaster gauze, laid up in sections as George Segal does. But remember this is not a true negative mold and is greatly wanting for fine detail.

Materials

Alginate, Cotton, (in roll form) Johnson & Johnson 4" Green label Plaster gauze, One of the following 3 cements: Plaster of Paris, Hydrocal, Ultracal 30, Hemp fibers, Plastic Buckets, A willing model.

The industry standard for lifecasting is dental Alginate. (pronounced Al-ja-net) Alginate is a completely organic, water activated seaweed derivative that creates tremendously detailed molds. (There are various silicones that are designed for casting from life but these are usually rather expensive.) Additionally, Alginate requires no release, which effectively eliminates the need for Vaseline and messy lubricants. The material is fast drying, clean, and with a little practice, relatively easy to use. There are many brand names for alginate: Just be sure to use a formula with a 3-4 minute gel time or longer. Gel time can be extended by using colder water. (Your models will love that!) There are also retarding agents available. Most dentists use a formula that gels in 60 seconds or less. This will be too fast for the techniques I will describe. My own preference is a Prosthetic Grade Cream by Alpha Dental.

A Word About Plaster Gauze

Generic aspirin has usually done the trick on my headaches and "brand X" mouthwash seems to keep my breath minty fresh. But when it comes to plaster gauze, there is no substitute for a brand name. The plaster gauze will be your "mother mold," and it must be fashioned and removed within 15 minutes. Don't sabotage your lifecast by using inferior materials. Johnson & Johnson plaster gauze (designed to set broken bones) is by far the best. The art store variety is inconsistent and often poorly packaged. The Johnson & Johnson brand is sealed sterile and airtight and works every time.

Preparation

It's a good idea to have all your supplies and tools laid out around you. You don't want any surprises while your model is panicking under a layer of goop. Let your machine take all calls and leave a note for the delivery man. Have all your plaster gauze pre-cut into 10 to 12 inch strips and your cotton laid out in sheets. Portion out enough alginate to do your pose, and have your ultracal pre-set in buckets. I always think of the cooking shows on television where everything is pre-measured in its own little container ready to be scooped up and thrown into the pan!

Choosing a Pose

Selecting a model and his or her pose will have a major influence on the outcome of your piece. Advertisers have known for years that youth and beauty directly impact the bottom line. So unless you are interested in a particular human abnormality, I suggest you start with an attractive model, and select a pose that is artistically strong. **Smaller areas are easier to master than larger areas.** Your mistakes will be smaller, too. Choose an area that is about 12" x 12". When you have mastered this scale, gradually extend your reach. Place your model in the position you would have gravity effect his body. Usually this means your model will be vertical. Make sure that an appropriate wall or apparatus is in place to support his pose. He will, after all, be under the knife for about twenty minutes. Leave as little to chance here as possible. Consider all the things that might go wrong. What can you do to minimize the model's discomfort?

Ready...Set...Go!

Your gauze is cut, your cotton is ready, and your model is in a zen-like trance. Spray the area to be cast with some cold water. The mist will reduce bubbles and shock your model into readiness. Begin adding cold water to the alginate. One formula recommends 17cc of water at 72 degrees to 50 gms. of alginate. *(Too much science takes the fun out of it, don't you think?)* Just run your tap water until it's as cold as possible and add it to the alginate, quickly mixing it to a consistency like runny oatmeal. Start with 1 part alginate to 1 part water by volume. You will probably want to add a little more water. Best advice...season to taste.

Scoop up the mix and flow it onto your model. Let gravity work to your advantage by starting at the top and allowing the mix to flow down. Really get in there and apply the stuff, don't just drip it on. Use your hands to "paint" the mix on every last square inch. Pat the surface to break any bubbles. On yeah, keep an eye on the clock. Tick-tick. *Remember: You have approximately 3 to 4 minutes to mix and apply the alginate. This is not a good time to check your notes.*

After the alginate has been applied to the model, but before it gels, you MUST push cotton fibers into the surface. Why? Alginate doesn't stick to anything and nothing really sticks to alginate. Consequently, the plaster gauze requires a bit of a nap so it can adhere. The cotton "embeds" in the alginate and the gauze sticks to the cotton. Make sure the cotton gets stuck at the edges! When the alginate has thoroughly gelled, you should remove the excess cotton, leaving only a light nap. (You will know when the alginate has gelled because it will peel off your hands like a pair of rubber gloves!) If your model appears to have been tarred and feathered, your on the right track.

Start applying the plaster gauze. I usually apply 3 to 4 strips at a time with the strips slightly fanned out. Dunk the the strips into a bucket of very **warm** water. (Plaster doesn't dry...it cures and heat accelerates the process.) Allow them to drain over the bucket and then apply them to the surface of the alginate and cotton. Again, don't just lay them on but really mold and conform the gauze to the surface of the alginate. The edges usually need a little reinforcement. Work quickly... your model is fading fast.

Removing the Mold

You've gotten this far so don't rush it now. Calmly loosen the alginate at the edges and ask the model to imagine his skin withdrawing from the inside. Slowly remove the mold from the model's body. The subject of body hair often comes up at this time. It would have been a very good idea for your model to have shaved!

Thank and pay your model and get him out of the way. You need to focus on the mold which must be cast right away. Alginate begins to dry out and break down quickly so it's time to start mixing cement.

Plaster of Paris vs. Hydrocal vs. Ultracal 30

All of these US Gypsum products are relatively cheap when purchased in 100lbs... bags but some will work better than others. Plaster of Paris is available everywhere but is very soft and chalky compared to the other materials. Hydrocal has a higher PSI rating and is probably a better material for a beginner. The big drawback is its high rate of expansion while curing. If you lay in gel coats of cement, which is a good idea, an expanding second layer tends to crack the first layer. Ultracal 30, which has an even higher PSI rating than Hydrocal, does not expand significantly while curing and allows for the gradual build up of several thin layers. Mix your cement to a creamy consistency. Again, you'll want to feel into what's right for you, but start with 2 parts cement to 1 part water by volume.

Often I lay my mold on pillows and boxes to cradle it. Fill or slurry your mold with cement. Use wire or hemp to reinforce larger pieces. Allow the piece to fully set, which is usually an hour or more.

The Unveiling

The mold you created is, in effect, a waste mold. You will need to tear, rip, crack, and break it off of your sculpture. Often it's easier to pull the shell off first and then begin tearing at the alginate. Your piece will probably need some touch ups. Fill voids with plaster or spackle and manicure other areas with a Dremmel tool.